T0328588

Cambridge Elements ≡

Elements in Political Economy
edited by
David Stasavage
New York University

DEMOCRATIZATION AND THE STATE

Competence, Control, and Performance in Indonesia's Civil Service

Jan H. Pierskalla
The Ohio State University

Shaftesbury Road, Cambridge CB2 8EA, United Kingdom

One Liberty Plaza, 20th Floor, New York, NY 10006, USA

477 Williamstown Road, Port Melbourne, VIC 3207, Australia

314–321, 3rd Floor, Plot 3, Splendor Forum, Jasola District Centre,
New Delhi – 110025, India

103 Penang Road, #05–06/07, Visioncrest Commercial, Singapore 238467

Cambridge University Press is part of Cambridge University Press & Assessment,
a department of the University of Cambridge.

We share the University's mission to contribute to society through the pursuit of
education, learning and research at the highest international levels of excellence.

www.cambridge.org
Information on this title: www.cambridge.org/9781009264815
DOI: 10.1017/9781009264839

First published 2022

A catalogue record for this publication is available from the British Library.

ISBN 978-1-009-26481-5 Paperback
ISSN 2398-4031 (online)
ISSN 2514-3816 (print)

Cambridge University Press & Assessment has no responsibility for the persistence
or accuracy of
URLs for external or third-party internet websites referred to in this publication
and does not guarantee that any content on such websites is, or will remain,
accurate or appropriate.

Democratization and the State

Competence, Control, and Performance in Indonesia's Civil Service

Elements in Political Economy

DOI: 10.1017/9781009264839
First published online: November 2022

Jan H. Pierskalla
The Ohio State University

Author for correspondence: Jan H. Pierskalla, Pierskalla.4@osu.edu

Abstract: Does democratization lead to more meritocracy in the civil service? The Element argues that electoral accountability increases the value of competence over personal loyalty in the civil service. While this resembles an application of merit principles, it does not automatically reduce patronage politics or improve public goods provision. Competent civil servants are often used to facilitate the distribution of clientelistic goods at mass scale to win competitive elections. The selection of competent but less loyal civil servants requires the increased use of control mechanisms, like the timing of promotions, to ensure their compliance. The Element tests these claims using novel micro-level data on promotions in Indonesia's civil service before and after democratization in 1999. The Element shows that national- and local-level elections led to increased promotion premiums for educated civil servants, and simultaneously generated electoral cycles in the timing of promotions, but did little to improve public goods provision.

The appendix for this Element can be found online at:
www.cambridge.org/appendix_democratization_and_the_state

Keywords: civil service, bureaucracy, meritocracy, patronage, democratization
JEL classifications: A12, B34, C56, D78, E90

ISBNs: 9781009264815 (PB), 9781009264839 (OC)
ISSNs: 2398-4031 (online), 2514-3816 (print)

Contents

1 Introduction   1

2 Democratization and the Management of the Civil
Service   12

3 Indonesia's Civil Service and the Transition to Democracy   22

4 Democratization, Competence, and Control   40

5 Democratization and Performance   67

6 Conclusion   90

References   95

A further Online Appendix can be accessed at
www.cambridge.org/Pierskalla_online_appendices

1 Introduction

What is the relationship between democratic accountability and state capacity? Does holding leaders accountable via elections improve the quality of state bureaucracies and the ability to govern? Or do elections hinder the creation of effective civil service organizations, and instead lead to a politicized bureaucracy, pervasive corruption, and clientelism? Modern and effective states are considered to be key to human flourishing. State capacity, or a state's *infrastructural power* (Mann, 1984; Soifer, 2008), describes its ability to "penetrate its territories and logistically implement decisions" (Mann, 1984, p. 183). Capable states have been associated with order and stability, economic development, better public goods provision, lower levels of corruption, and higher degrees of perceived legitimacy.[1] Effective state bureaucracies are integral for state capacity (Evans & Rauch, 1999): they project the state's infrastructural power across its territory and serve as its key interface with the general population.

Although modern states have violent histories and coercive origins (Mann, 1986; Scott, 2017; Tilly, 1990), they are powerful organizing tools for human societies that enhance their collective problem-solving capacity. An array of pressing governance challenges – ranging from the provision of basic services like health care, education, policing, and infrastructure to addressing new and complex issues such as climate change, global pandemics, and the regulation of large technology companies or financial markets – can benefit from effective and competent state action.

At a descriptive level, indicators of human well-being strongly correlate with measures of state capacity. Figure 1 illustrates this for the relationship between state fiscal capacity and (logged) GDP per capita for 179 countries in 2015.[2] Fiscal capacity is a key component of infrastructural power (Mann, 1984; Soifer, 2008), which captures the state's ability to extract economic resources from the population to finance its own activities. As Figure 1 illustrates, countries that feature a strong fiscal infrastructure (such as personal income taxes and value-added tax) are, on average, much richer than those that do not. An

---

[1] See, for example, Bockstette, Chanda, & Putterman (2002); Evans & Rauch (1999); Pepinsky, Pierskalla, & Sacks (2017); Rauch & Evans (2000); Soifer (2008).

[2] I use the Varieties of Democracy (V-Dem) (Coppedge et al., 2019) measure of fiscal capacity, which asks expert coders to rate a country's fiscal capacity from 0 ("The state is not capable of raising revenue to finance itself") to 4 ("The state primarily relies on taxes on economic transactions (such as sales taxes) and/or taxes on income, corporate profits and capital"). Expert scores are aggregated via a Bayesian item response theory measurement model, scaled to mean 0.

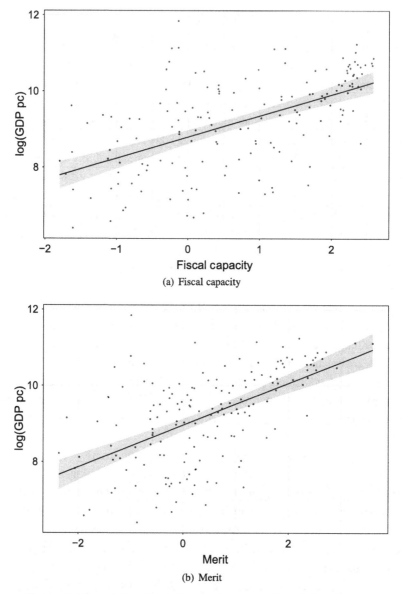

(a) Fiscal capacity

(b) Merit

Figure 1 The relationship between state capacity and development
Note: Panel (a) displays a bivariate scatterplot between V-Dem's fiscal
capacity measure and logged GDP per capita. Panel (b) displays a bivariate
scatterplot between V-Dem's measure of meritocratic recruitment in the civil
service and logged GDP per capita.

effective state apparatus – in the form of a modern, meritocratic bureaucracy –
has also been considered a key contributor to infrastructural power (Mann,
1984; Soifer, 2008) since at least Weber (1978). Panel (b) of Figure 1 shows
the bivariate scatterplot for the relationship between meritocratic recruitment in

the civil service and (logged) GDP per capita in 2015.[3] Again, there is a strong cross-country correlation between the degree of meritocracy in a country's civil service and its level of economic development. These bivariate correlations are confirmed in more involved regression analyses.[4] While it is difficult to determine the direction of causality of these broad patterns (see, e.g., Cornell, Knutsen, & Teorell [2020] for a skeptical perspective), many experts, scholars, and practitioners believe that commanding a capable state apparatus yields substantial benefits for human well-being.

Historically, scholars have disagreed over the exact relationship between democracy and state capacity (see Gjerløw et al. [2021] for a comprehensive and up-to-date review). Some take an optimistic view: elections make leaders responsive to voters, and voters want the state to solve problems, ergo politicians have an incentive to build better bureaucracies to fulfill their political promises. According to that perspective, modern, competent Weberian bureaucracies – insulated from excessive political meddling but responsive to elected leaders' priorities – are a perfect complement to mass democracy.[5] Democratization thus gives political leaders an incentive to improve the performance of the state writ large, including its bureaucratic apparatus. Some empirical evidence seems to support this optimistic view of democratization, such as finding a link between democratic competition and higher-quality government or the passage of civil service reform laws that formally enshrine meritocratic principles.[6] Descriptively, indicators of democracy and measures of state capacity correlate quite strongly. Figure 2 displays the bivariate scatterplot between V-Dem's measure of electoral democracy (*polyarchy*, ranging

---

[3] V-Dem (Coppedge et al., 2019) also provides information on meritocratic recruitment to the civil service. Expert coders rate a country's recruitment practices from 0 ("All appointment decisions in the state administration are based on personal or political connections. None are based on skills and merit") to 4 ("None of the appointment decisions in the state administration are based on personal or political connections. All are based on skills and merit"). As with the fiscal capacity measure, expert scores are aggregated via a Bayesian item response theory measurement model, scaled to mean 0.

[4] In Appendix A. All appendices can be found online at https://janpierskalla.files.wordpress.com/2022/09/appendix__democratization_and_the_state.pdf, I report the results of a simple exercise that explores the relationship between fiscal capacity and meritocracy in the civil service and economic development in a panel regression framework. Controlling for a variety of confounders, measures of state capacity are positively correlated with GDP per capita. The analysis includes country and year fixed effects, as well as controls for urbanization level, population size, electoral democracy, and international and domestic armed conflict. See details in Appendix A.

[5] Stasavage (2020) points out that this complementarity between mass democracy and a strong, competent state bureaucracy is a decidedly modern pairing.

[6] See, for example, Geddes (1994); Giovanni & Vincenzo (2015); Grundholm & Thorsen (2019); Grzymala-Busse (2007); Theriault (2003); Wang & Xu (2018).

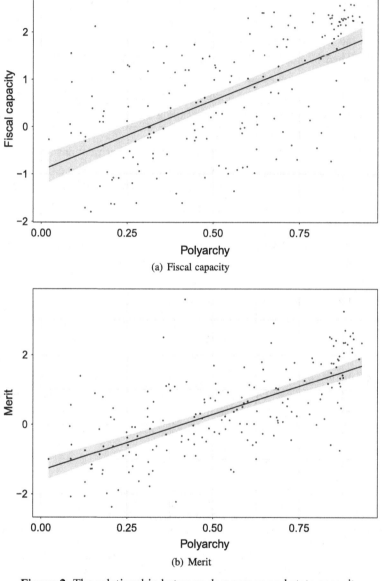

Figure 2 The relationship between democracy and state capacity
Note: Panel (a) displays a bivariate scatterplot between V-Dem's electoral
democracy measure and fiscal capacity; Panel (b) displays a bivariate
scatterplot between V-Dem's electoral democracy measure and meritocratic
recruitment in the civil service.

from 0 to 1) (Coppedge et al., 2019) and the measures of fiscal capacity (Panel
(a)) and meritocracy (Panel (b)).

Others have been more skeptical about whether democracy improves public
sector performance. For instance, Huntington (1968) warned about the dangers

of premature democratization before states are fully consolidated. Introducing competitive elections before a strong and effective state has emerged may hinder (or even reverse) the state-building process. Politicians in democracies, facing competitive pressures, may use the state as a political resource – cannibalizing it to bestow rents on supporters and cater to particularistic interests. Elections in developing democracies might be more realistically characterized by the prevalence of clientelistic rather than programmatic politics, which forces politicians to leverage their control over the state to increase patronage hiring and wasteful expenditures to win competitive elections.[7] From that perspective, competitive elections may sometimes weaken state capacity – specifically the state apparatus.

Understanding the relationship between democratic accountability and state-building – and which sequence of reforms maximizes the likelihood of consolidating accountable *and* effective government – is an important research puzzle. If we want democracy to deliver on governance, that is, to improve the lives of ordinary people, we need to examine the triangular relationship between citizens, rulers, and bureaucrats that determines state performance. I contend that we can make substantial headway on this puzzle by acknowledging that *people make the state.*

Often, when we think of state capacity and the emergence of effective states, this brings to mind the state's power to coerce. Enforcing the monopoly of violence is widely regarded as the defining feature of states. We may also consider the state's ability to collect taxes from (and accurate information about) citizens, that is, making the social and economic world legible in order to extract and compel. States' capacity to accomplish such tasks is borne out of a long and protracted state-building process, which is driven by violent conflict (Tilly, 1990), competition, and emulation and learning (Huang & Kang, 2022), the incremental efforts of violent elites to impose political order (Olson, 1993), bargains between rulers and powerful elite groups (Stasavage, 2020), and technological advancements (Cermeño, Enflo, & Lindvall, 2022).[8]

While these deep structural explanations of state capacity provide powerful insights into the origins of modern states and their bureaucratic apparatus, they also obscure the fact that the challenge of human resource management, that is, *how people make the state*, lies at the heart of state governance. State agents carry out the many functions that states provide; in essence, they are the vectors

---

[7] See, for example, Driscoll (2017); Grzymala-Busse (2007); O'Dwyer (2004); Pierskalla & Sacks (2020); Schuster (2018).

[8] For example, writing, Roman roads, gunpowder, the printing press, the railroad, the telegraph, and changes in agricultural technology have all drastically altered central states' ability to govern the periphery.

of state power. They work as bureaucrats and civil servants, ranging from front-line service providers to high-level officials. These individuals – embedded within a formal organizational structure – constitute the mundane machinery of abstract state power. Who these state agents are and how they are managed matters.[9]

Rulers who want to establish political order over people and territory must delegate the daily tasks of governance to these agents. To understand state capacity and power, we therefore need to examine how political leaders manage these agents. The history of state-building can be thought of as the evolving set of answers to two questions asked by aspiring political rulers: Who should I recruit to act on my behalf? How should I manage them? The answers reveal much about the state's shape, structure, operation, and relationship with its citizens.[10]

If we start by observing that people make the state, we can then explore how different kinds of political regimes provide incentives to address the state's human resources management challenges. Leaders use the state to do a lot of things: collect taxes, enforce laws, educate people, build roads, run the postal system, provide health care, and regulate a variety of economic sectors. Depending on the political incentives and the problems they face, some rulers also use it to spy on citizens; imprison, torture and murder, expropriate citizens; siphon money toward offshore bank accounts; and reward supporters. Political survival is a key organizing feature of the political world and shapes the principal–agent problems inherent in the state bureaucracy.

I argue that some of the disagreement over how democratization shapes the state stems from an insufficient distinction between how such a transition affects *how civil servants are managed* and how it affects *what purposes they are used for*. I argue that introducing electoral competition has a *selection-for-competence* effect in everyday civil service management practices. In many authoritarian regimes, civil servants are selected and elevated to positions of influence based on their personal connections to the dictator's inner circle and their *incompetence*, which makes them less likely to betray the ruler (a *selection-for-loyalty* effect or *cronyism*) (Egorov & Sonin, 2011; Zakharov, 2016; Zudenkova, 2015). The prevalence of cronyism makes autocratic civil

---

[9] Take, for example, research by Best, Hjort, & Szakonyi (2019). Studying public procurement in Russia, they provide a high-quality, quantitative estimate of the importance of individual bureaucrat quality: they estimate that 40 percent of the variation in quality-adjusted prices paid during procurement processes is due to individual bureaucrats and their management.

[10] Hassan (2020) provides a wonderful example of this kind of approach in the context of authoritarian rule. She documents the various ways in which Kenyan leaders have used decisions about hiring, posting, shuffling, and promoting civil servants to achieve regime goals.

service organizations safe for dictators. It makes them willing to use repression to squash popular opposition at the behest of leadership (Scharpf & Gläßel, 2020) and good at offering rent-seeking opportunities to a small number of insiders, but less effective at public goods provision or mass-level machine politics.

Moving from autocracy to a system with competitive elections provides incentives to abandon this narrow form of cronyism. Once political elites have to win a majority of votes in competitive elections, competent civil servants become more valuable. Skilled civil servants can be deployed to provide goods preferred by voters, including better public goods and services, but also (and more likely in a developing democracy) distribute targeted benefits at the mass level (Keefer, 2007).

This *selection-for-competence* effect of democratization does not, by itself, produce uniform effects on the *quality* of public goods provision. This is because whether politicians direct civil servants to improve the delivery of public goods or engage in machine politics is determined by the sociopolitical context in which elections take place and the extent to which there exists a trade-off between clientelism and public goods delivery. In many low-income democracies, clientelistic appeals may be more advantageous to politicians due to the prevalence of poverty (Weitz-Shapiro, 2012) and the lack of programmatic credibility (Keefer & Vlaicu, 2007). Competence can be useful for either programmatic politics or clientelism. Moreover, patronage politics can, under some circumstances, improve government performance (Jiang, 2018; Toral, 2021). Thus the increased competence in the civil service induced by democratic accountability may lead to better public goods, more effective patronage politics, or both, depending on the local electoral environment.

Electoral accountability also generates a secondary effect: an increased tendency to select competent but less *personally* loyal civil servants requires politicians to exercise more active *control* over the bureaucracy to ensure the delivery of government goods and services at electorally beneficial times. Competence often comes at the price of control. When leaders cannot rely on the intrinsic loyalty of their agents, they have to engage in costly and imperfect reward and sanctioning tools, for example, offering promotions and rent-seeking opportunities or threatening dismissals and transfers to undesirable locations or work duties. While all leaders have to develop techniques of control,[11] electoral accountability amplifies the challenge of control and ties it

---

[11] For example, Hassan (2020) describes how autocratic rulers in Kenya use their ability to shuffle bureaucrats across districts to manage the problem of disloyal agents. Similarly, De Juan, Krautwald, & Pierskalla (2017) study agency problems in the management of colonial police

to the electoral calendar. The high stakes of competitive elections often engender the politicization of everyday management practices in the bureaucracy, tying the career fortunes of civil servants to the political survival of elected politicians. Due to the importance of promotions in hierarchical civil service organizations for affecting bureaucratic effort (Bertrand et al., n.d.; Karachiwalla & Park, 2017), politicians will leverage their control over the timing of promotions to affect their political fortunes, inducing electoral cycles in otherwise routine civil service promotion procedures.

This second observable implication is more pronounced in environments where electoral competition is characterized by *clientelistic* appeals. Delivering particularistic goods to benefit politicians requires more ad hoc intervention in the management of bureaucrats in such contexts. Yet when electoral competition is structured by *programmatic* appeals, politicians still value the ability to exercise direct control over civil servants, but are more willing to make an institutional commitment to an autonomous Weberian-style civil service. A Weberian state combines a preference for competence with a commitment to a depoliticized management style, in essence granting increased autonomy to the civil service, limiting political leaders' ability to directly meddle in the internal processes of the state apparatus. Democratization then represents somewhat of a poisoned chalice with respect to the goal of a Weberian state – it generates a strong incentive to increase *competence*, but that same incentive also creates a need for increased political *control*.

In sum, my argument links democratization to *who* is selected for top civil service posts and *how* they are managed. It also implies important boundary conditions. Democratization will generate the hypothesized effects when transitioning from a system that heavily relied on cronyism, which does not characterize all authoritarian regimes. For example, a competitive authoritarian regime (Levitsky & Way, 2010) may have already adopted similar practices even before democratization.

Studying the relationship between regime change and the state bureaucracy is challenging for at least two reasons. First, it is difficult to determine how democratization affects the quality of the state bureaucracy due to concerns of reverse causality and confounding. For example, the level of state capacity may be driving democratization rather than the other way around. In addition, other factors, such as the level of economic development, may affect both the likelihood of adopting modern bureaucratic structures *and* democratic political

---

forces, identifying the trade-offs in assigning agents to locations with more or less central oversight.

institutions. Classic cross-national work typically cannot narrowly identify the causal effect of democracy on state capacity. The second challenge is that empirical work, especially cross-national studies, typically has to rely on fairly crude indicators of a state's bureaucratic characteristics that are too coarse to accurately capture the dynamics I have outlined.

To address both concerns, I test my argument using Indonesia's transition to democracy in 1999 as my case study. President Suharto's authoritarian New Order regime ruled the country for more than thirty years, relying on the support of the military, the ruling Golkar party, and the Indonesian civil service. Civil servants were tasked with (and rewarded for) executing the will of the autocratic leadership, which ranged from collecting taxes, executing laws, and providing public goods to spying on their fellow citizens, denying access to government services based on political allegiances, and facilitating rent seeking by regime insiders. The country's unexpected transition to democracy in 1999 placed electorally accountable political leaders in charge of the vast civil service, making this a relevant and instructive case.

Causal identification in this case is aided by the unexpected nature of the transition in 1999 and the additional, staggered introduction of competitive direct elections for local government offices after 2005 (Pierskalla & Sacks, 2018; Skoufias et al., 2014). This allows me to exploit the exogenous nature of the national and local roll-out of competitive elections to study their effects on the management of the Indonesian civil service.

A second advantage of using Indonesia as a case study is the rich administrative data available. I draw on the full administrative records of Indonesia's four million currently active civil servants and their career histories from 1980 to 2015, to assess how educational attainment and election cycles affected their chances of promotion before and after democratization. This allows me to investigate, at the micro level, whether the macro-institutional change in 1999 affected management *practices* in the country's civil service. While changes to formal institutions such as laws, regulations, and procedures are important, they are neither necessary nor sufficient for the actual practice of meritocracy in the civil service (Schuster, 2017). I investigate actual promotion decisions to determine the revealed preferences governing decision-making in the civil service. This approach avoids the risk of being misled by de jure changes that have no meaningful practical implications and are merely a form of ineffectual "institutional mimicry" (Andrews, Pritchett, & Woolcock, 2017).

I test whether democratization affected the promotion premium associated with civil servants' educational attainment – a common metric used to indicate employees' ability and skill (Card, 1999), which has been found to increase the productivity of politicians (Martinez-Bravo, 2017) and civil servants (He & Wang, 2017).[12] I expect highly educated civil servants to advance faster and further in their careers after democratization than under autocratic rule because the electoral incentives under democratic rule favor competence. Given Indonesia's electoral environment and the prevalence of clientelism, I also expect that the increase in *selection for competence* at the expense of personal loyalty requires politicians to mitigate principal–agent problems in the management of civil servants. This should be expressed in the timing of promotions in election years under democratic – but not autocratic – rule.

I estimate the effects of educational attainment and election timing on civil servants' chances of promotion in an individual-level difference-in-differences setting. I find strong and robust evidence that the premium for educational attainment substantially increased after democratization. A civil servant with a postgraduate degree was twice as likely to be promoted under democracy as under autocratic rule. The introduction of district-level elections generated a similar pattern. Democratization pushed the Indonesian bureaucracy toward rewarding competence. Parallel to the increased premium for education, I document the emergence of electoral cycles: promotions are more strongly tied to the electoral calendar under democratic than autocratic rule. The strength of these effects varies according to the dominance of the state apparatus in the local economy, which tracks with the prevalence of clientelism in Indonesia (Aspinall & Berenschot, 2019). This is consistent with a corresponding need for political control, resulting in an increasingly politicized civil service.

In addition to analyzing individual civil servant careers, I also explore the downstream consequences of democratization in 1999 on the quality of public goods delivery, corruption, and perceptions of the state in Indonesia. My argument suggests that the *selection-for-competence* effect of democratization does not necessarily translate to improved public goods provision. Using aggregate national-level data, I show that overall public service delivery and experts' perceptions of the quality of governance have improved since 1999, but there is no strong evidence that this is due to democratization alone. At the local level, there is some empirical evidence that electoral competition has increased government expenditures as well as some indicators of the quality of the service provision, especially in regions where electoral accountability is paired with competence in the civil service. However, democratization has been linked to a worrying trend toward decentralized forms of corruption and intense politicization of the state apparatus.

---

[12] Education is a common proxy for quality in the literature on political candidates (Besley & Reynal-Querol, 2011; Ferraz & Finan, 2011).

My research makes three primary contributions. First, understanding the conditions under which capable "Weberian" bureaucracies have emerged throughout history is one of the most important questions in comparative politics. Well-known theories emphasize long, historical processes of incremental state-building, driven by the threat of war for instance (Tilly, 1990). My approach emphasizes the importance of studying the human resources dimension of state capacity, to help appreciate the political incentives governing actual management practices in the state bureaucracy. *People* make the state just as much as war does.

Second, I build on prior work that focuses on how democratization and electoral competition affect the civil service (Geddes, 1994). My findings suggest that democratization has meaningful effects on the role of meritocracy in the civil service, and identify a selection-for-competence effect that is conceptually distinct from the quality of outputs produced by the state. While democratization gives political leaders incentives to reward competence within the civil service, it also drives them toward exerting more direct control, politicizing the bureaucracy, and has uncertain downstream implications for the quality of governance and public goods provision. My findings suggest that researchers must carefully evaluate how competence affects the levels of corruption and patronage in developing countries' civil services. Competence may simultaneously facilitate better public goods provision, more efficient corruption, and large-scale patronage (for a related point, see Weaver [2021]). Likewise, increased control by politicians can be used to reduce particular forms of bureaucratic corruption *or* to sustain mass-level machine politics.[13] Consequently, reforms that reward the recruitment and promotion of civil servants based on standard metrics of competence – for example, performance pay systems – have to consider the larger political context to assess the downstream effects on the quality of government.

In a third contribution, this study is one of the first to draw on micro-level administrative data on the full population of civil servants from a developing country, covering a time period before and after democratization. As such, it offers a unique and completely novel empirical view of micro-level changes in a state's bureaucracy during regime changes. Related studies by Bhavnani & Lee (2017), Gulzar & Pasquale (2017), and Hassan (2020) equally show the benefit of using large-scale, micro-level administrative data on the state itself to

---

[13] Complementary work by Valsecchi (2016) evaluates the relationship between reelection incentives, corruption, and promotions in the Indonesian civil service using aggregate district-level data from 2002 to 2011. He finds that reelection incentives lead to lower observed rates of corruption among Indonesian bureaucrats, driven by more active management interventions from politicians.

shed light on perennial questions about state capacity, responsive government, and representation.

2 Democratization and the Management of the Civil Service

Scholars of state capacity have tried to bring conceptual and empirical clarity to the notion of strong and effective states (Berwick & Christia, 2016; Hendrix, 2010; Soifer, 2008). Strong states can draw on infrastructural power: they have the ability to implement political decisions across their territory and, more or less, ensure compliance by the governed population (Mann, 1984; Soifer, 2008). Soifer (2008) clarifies that infrastructural power can be assessed as a state's national capabilities, such as its ability to raise revenue or the size of its national army, but also relates to its territorial reach – penetrating the geographic, economic, and social peripheries – and its effect on and relationship with society. Observationally, infrastructural power has been tied to measures of extractive, coercive, and administrative capacity (Hanson & Sigman, 2021), including the ability to collect information on (and monitor) the population (Brambor et al., 2020; Lee & Zhang, 2016).

The "iron cage" of bureaucracy cuts across these dimensions (Mann, 1984). Ever since centralized political hierarchies in the form of states emerged, rulers have had to assign the actual duties of governance to agents (Scott, 2017). No ruler exerts power alone; centralized political regimes have to rely on organizational structures. Rulers need to decide which tasks are delegated to which agent, and how to manage this ongoing relationship. Infrastructural power is, in many ways, actualized and exerted via the management of people: *people make the state*. I believe a productive way to understand state capacity is to unpack the ways in which different rulers have delegated governance tasks to bureaucratic agents.

Modern states use professional bureaucracies to carry out this delegation task; they have a hierarchical structure, specialized tasks and responsibilities, legally formalized procedures, detailed record-keeping practices, and a competent, permanent workforce (Weber, 1978). Contemporary scholars, experts, and policy-makers agree, in principle, on the core components of professionalization – formalized entrance exams, secure tenure, nonpoliticized jobs, and civil servant recruitment and management decisions based on merit – although many real-world bureaucracies fall short of that ideal (Raadschelders, Vigoda-Gadot, & Kisner, 2015; Rauch & Evans, 2000). The idea of meritocracy in particular has become integral, even synonymous, with a modern "Weberian" bureaucracy, and has been directly linked to the delivery of public services, growth, better governance, and improvements in human welfare (see, e.g., Evans & Rauch [1999]; Meyer-Sahling, Mikkelsen, & Schuster [2018]; Pepinsky, Pierskalla, and Sacks [2017]).

Weberian, meritocratic bureaucracies are a fairly recent phenomenon. State bureaucracies typically grew out of rulers' personal staff and traditionally represented pure patronage positions (Grindle, 2012). Rulers relied on their personal, familial, and extended networks to identify, recruit, and control candidates for key state positions. The principal–agent problems inherent to the delegation of state functions were managed not via formalized procedures, the inculcation of an *esprit de corps*, or bureaucratic monitoring and sanctioning technologies, but by relying on personal loyalty and mutually beneficial patronage. Modern bureaucratic apparatuses only gradually de-emphasized civil servants' personal loyalty to the ruler.[14]

The literature identifies several reasons for the development of modern Weberian bureaucracies. Most prominently, *bellicist* theories emphasize the need to generate revenue (see, e.g., Dincecco [2015]) and the threat of war (Tilly, 1990) as core drivers of the development of capable state bureaucracies in Western Europe. A lack of fiscal resources, paired with geopolitical insecurity and credible internal threats from the masses, is also associated with the deliberate construction of a legal–rational civil service in East and Southeast Asia (Doner, Ritchie, & Slater, 2005). Others have focused on specific colonial legacies as a potential origin of capable state bureaucracies (Kohli, 2004).

How does political regime type shape the incentives to adopt a meritocratic approach to managing the state bureaucracy? Democratization entails a variety of institutional, political, and social changes, but at its core requires a change in the rules of leadership selection: a move to competitive elections. Competitive, free, and fair elections are the cornerstone of democratic accountability and dramatically affect rulers' incentive structures. Elections provide a mechanism to hold leaders accountable and make public policy responsive to voter preferences (Besley, 2006). How does electoral accountability and voter responsiveness relate to more meritocracy in the civil service? For one, voters may inherently desire a meritocratic civil service. Voters may prefer a rules-based, neutral, and reliable bureaucracy and could use the power of their vote to affect that change. More realistically, even if regular voters have no strong feelings on the role of meritocracy in the civil service, their desire for improved public goods provision and general welfare generates a performance incentive for politicians (Besley & Burgess, 2002; Stasavage, 2005). By extension, this

---

[14] China is a notable exception: it employed civil service entrance exams for over 1,300 years (Bai & Jia, 2016).

performance incentive has implications for bureaucracy, because it increases the value of meritocratic practices to leaders relative to patronage and cronyism when managing the civil service.

If voters demand better public services, politicians have an incentive to build an effective state apparatus that can deliver them in core areas like health care, education, and basic infrastructure. An effective state apparatus is typically characterized by the application of meritocratic principles (Evans & Rauch, 1999; Rauch & Evans, 2000).[15] Hence, the threat of losing competitive elections may make politicians more likely to enshrine meritocratic norms and practices in the civil service because this helps ensure they have the tools to deliver public goods effectively at scale.[16] Callen and colleagues (2016) illustrate this type of incentive effect at the micro level. They report the results of a field experiment that increased government inspectors' ability to observe doctors' absenteeism by equipping them with a smartphone monitoring system (i.e., increasing state capacity). This system reduced absentee rates among monitored doctors in areas with competitive elections, where political incentives aligned with bureaucratic capacity to improve outcomes. At the macro level, several empirical studies have found a positive association between democracy and meritocratic laws and practices in the civil service,[17] democracy and administrative capacity,[18] and between democratization, suffrage extensions, competitive elections, and public goods provision.[19]

Competitive elections can also encourage meritocracy in the civil service for more mundane reasons, such as denying political rivals control over future bureaucratic spoils (Ting et al., 2013). This logic can also explain why politicians sometimes support the passage of freedom of information and anti-corruption laws: they seek to limit future opportunities for patronage and corruption (Berliner & Erlich, 2015; Grzymala-Busse, 2006). Competitive elections may also strengthen the state through infrastructural mechanisms: holding elections

---

[15] Stasavage (2020) points out that this combination of competitive mass elections and a meritocratic, capable state is an entirely modern phenomenon. Historically, democracy thrived in weak states, while authoritarian rule relied on early forms of strong bureaucratic structures (Stasavage, 2020).

[16] Harding and Stasavage (2014) provide an important addendum to this logic: in the short run, politicians may focus on policies that are easily observable by voters and shy away from long-term investments.

[17] See, for example, Geddes (1994); Horn (1995); Ruhil & Camões (2003); Theriault (2003); Ting et al. (2013); Wang & Xu (2018).

[18] See, for example, Giovanni & Vincenzo (2015); Grundholm & Thorsen (2019); Wang & Xu (2018).

[19] See, for example, Besley & Burgess (2002); Fujiwara (2015); Gerring, Thacker, & Alfaro (2012); Kudamatsu (2012); Stasavage (2005).

requires registering voters, which increases the local presence of the state and the legibility of the population (Slater, 2008).

While normatively appealing, others are skeptical of the effects of democratization on bureaucracy (Huntington, 1968). A number of authors have argued that electoral competition can sometimes intensify patronage and bloat in the public sector and weaken overall state capacity.[20] Building on this strand of the literature, I argue that democratization does not cause either merit *or* patronage in the civil service. I develop a new argument that offers more specific predictions about how it affects the preferred traits of top-level civil servants as well as promotion decisions. My argument produces observable implications about *who* is likely to be considered for top positions in the civil service and *when* promotions happen relative to the electoral calendar.

I draw on the formal literature on the *loyalty–competence trade-off*, which has developed in the context of authoritarian politics. Like all rulers, autocrats must delegate tasks to members of the civil service. This applies to standard government functions, like taxation, education, and health care, as well as tasks specific to autocratic regimes, such as repressing opposition forces or appropriating economic resources. Unlike leaders in democracies, dictators have to worry about violent challenges from regime insiders (Svolik, 2012), which generates a trade-off for authoritarian rulers (Egorov & Sonin, 2011; Zakharov, 2016; Zudenkova, 2015). Dictators need capable civil servants who can implement their policy agenda. But capable agents represent a risk because they can expect to be in high demand from potential rival rulers, or could themselves build independent bases of power in the state apparatus from which to launch a challenge to the ruler. For example, a dictator who selects a capable individual to run the secret police will benefit from the reduced likelihood of a successful mass uprising. However, the head of the police is one of the most dangerous potential rivals of the incumbent ruler (Svolik, 2013). This dilemma leads many autocratic rulers to favor mediocre or even incompetent – but *loyal* – civil servants (such as personal cronies or family members).[21] A personally loyal but low-quality civil servant is of little value to a challenger, and hence has nothing to gain from a regime change; nor are they likely to build an independent base of power within the bureaucracy. This trade-off might be particularly pronounced in times of threat or crisis (Aaskoven & Nyrup, 2021).

---

[20] See, for example, Bäck & Hadenius (2008); Driscoll (2017); Grzymala-Busse (2007); O'Dwyer (2004); Schuster (2020).

[21] Lee and Schuler (2020) further distinguish between technical and political competence; the latter represents the greatest threat to authoritarian rulers.

This preference for personal loyalty contrasts starkly with the ideal-type Weberian bureaucracy, which is characterized by loyalty to the rule of law, bureaucratic procedure, and allegiance to the *office* of the executive – not the individual occupying it.[22]

Thus civil service organizations in many autocratic regimes are characterized by *cronyism* – favoring personal loyalty over competence. Civil servants in crony regimes are less likely to be qualified for their job (see, e.g., the selection of low-quality recruits into Argentina's secret police as documented by Scharpf & Gläßel [2020]). Such regimes are also less likely to have high levels of competence in the delivery of public goods and services at the mass level (Dahlstrohm & Lapuente, 2017).

While the logic of the loyalty–competence trade-off may not extend across all levels of the hierarchy of the civil service, for example, the recruitment of frontline service providers is likely to be shaped less by loyalty concerns, it bears important implications for mid- to high-level management positions, that is, positions of power and influence with substantial rent-seeking opportunities. Moreover, the loyalty–competence trade-off does not have to be restricted to only the dictator and their immediate cronies, but may replicate at lower levels of the regime's hierarchy, that is, *cronies of cronies*. Since violence and extralegal means remain an option for resolving power struggles within hierarchical structures of authoritarian regimes, mid-level functionaries also have to worry about the loyalty of *their* agents.

What happens when crony authoritarian regimes transition to democracy and the leaders in charge of the civil service must suddenly compete in elections? I argue that such a transition does not automatically lead to the creation of a perfect Weberian bureaucracy and improved public goods provision. Rather, after democratization, leaders shift their political strategy from maintaining a small ruling coalition to winning a majority of votes in competitive elections. While this would ideally require improving the provision of public goods, prior research on clientelism (Hicken, 2011; Keefer, 2007; Kitschelt & Wilkinson, 2007) makes clear that candidates can win elections in young democracies by providing targeted private goods in clientelistic exchanges. This is especially likely when politicians lack the credibility for programmatic politics (Keefer,

---

[22] A similar debate about the role of competence and political loyalty has emerged with respect to the selection of *political cadres*, as opposed to civil servants, in authoritarian regimes (see, e.g., Gueorguiev & Schuler [2016]; Reuter & Robertson [2012]). The selection of political decision-makers also seems be subject to a loyalty–competence trade-off. The literature on cadre selection in China, for instance, provides evidence of the importance of cadre performance *and* factional affiliation as criteria for advancement (e.g., Jia, Kudamatsu, & Seim [2015]; Shih, Adolph, & Liu [2012]; Xu [2011]).

2007). The state bureaucracy, however, often facilitates and aids clientelistic politics (Oliveros, 2021). If an authoritarian system has relied on cronyism to stay in power, its civil service will be ill-equipped to provide programmatic public goods or mass-level clientelism. Autocratic leaders have to focus on keeping a small group of cronies happy, with little consideration for the broader population. Yet winning elections, even in a clientelistic environment, requires the mass distribution of goods and services. This increases the value of *competent* over merely *personally loyal* civil servants. Competent civil servants can coordinate the deployment of public resources in the service of a political machine. Thus democratization *does* increase the role of merit in the bureaucracy – in the narrow dimension of valuing the ability of individual civil servants. It does not mean that democratization reduces the discretionary control over the civil service (in fact, often the opposite); nor does it necessitate that competent civil servants are used to improve public goods. Studying bureaucratic hiring practices in Ghana, Brierley (2020) shows that in patronage-ridden environments, patrons value skill in high-ranking positions and limit the distribution of menial government jobs as a form of patronage.

What do democratization and its associated demand for competence imply for the day-to-day management of the civil service? Observationally, I expect democratization to increase the promotion of civil servants with characteristics that proxy for competence, such as educational attainment, that is, a *selection-for-competence* effect,[23] whether elections are characterized by programmatic or clientelistic appeals.

Main hypothesis: Democratization increases the promotion premium of competence.

However, this promotion premium for competence does not automatically imply a reduction of corruption or patronage, because individual civil servant competence is not necessarily at odds with systematic corruption or patronage. For example, a recent study of civil servants in the health sector of a low-income country found an empirical correlation between competence and corruption: the individuals who paid the largest bribes to acquire a civil service position were also the most capable (Weaver, 2021). Similarly, Jiang, Shao, & Zhang (2022) argue that anti-corruption efforts may dissuade high-quality candidates from entering the civil service.

I remain agnostic about the overall downstream effects of democratization on the civil service's ability to provide public goods and improve citizen welfare.

---

[23] Section 4 discusses the use of educational attainment as a proxy for competence.

In some contexts, its *selection-for-competence* effect will translate to improved public goods provision. When the electoral environment favors politicians and parties with programmatic platforms, competent civil servants will be directed to increase the mass delivery of widely accessible public programs. When the electoral environment favors voter linkages based on clientelistic appeals, politicians will instruct competent civil servants to engage in mass-level machine politics. The latter will not necessarily enhance service delivery; it may instead lead to more waste and misappropriation of resources – although evidence from China suggests that even patronage politics can improve government performance when it mitigates principal–agent problems (Jiang, 2018). Work by Toral (2021) also suggests that bureaucrats embedded in patronage networks may improve their performance due to stronger upward ties that unlock material and nonmaterial resources.

While the downstream consequences of the quality of public goods provision may depend on the context, electoral competition generates additional implications for managing civil servants. When electoral outcomes are uncertain, politicians may want to expand their discretional control over the civil service (Schuster, 2018). This aspect of my argument produces additional observable implications about the *timing* of promotions. If democratization enhances the value of competent over personally loyal civil servants, politicians must acknowledge that competent civil servants are not inherently loyal to particularistic political goals. This makes the nature of the relationship between politicians and bureaucrats more transactional: politicians must rely on something other than personal loyalty to exercise control over the behavior and allegiance of competent civil servants. This generates classic principal–agent problems that can be addressed using a variety of monitoring and sanctioning tools.[24]

I focus here on one specific tool: the timing of promotions. Given the starkly hierarchical nature of state bureaucracies, decisions about promotions to senior posts are one of the most important levers to influence the behavior of civil servants; they affect the overall operation of the civil service (Bertrand et al., n.d.; Karachiwalla & Park, 2017). If civil service promotions are used to build clientelistic political machines that are skilled at providing targeted benefits to large swathes of voters, politicians have to link rewards to civil servants'

---

[24] Note that autocrats also have to think about ways to manage civil servants to further regime goals, and can rely more often on loyalty. For instance, Hassan (2020) offers a thoughtful account of the various ways in which Kenyan autocratic leaders have used their discretion over posting decisions to mitigate regime threats, especially for bureaucrats who lack signifiers of regime loyalty. Studying German colonial police forces in Namibia, De Juan, Krautwald, & Pierskalla (2017) also investigate the control of post assignments as a management tool.

display of effort. This is most important in election years, when politicians are crucially dependent on civil servants' support. Qualitative case studies from Indonesia suggest that bureaucrats are often strategically transferred, shuffled, and promoted during election campaigns to ensure their political support.[25]

To facilitate clientelistic exchanges, politicians reward key civil servants with promotions before or after the election, depending on how credible bargains can be arranged.[26] While prior studies disagree on the specific conditions under which rewards (or sanctions) should be provided before or after an election, at a minimum, this dynamic will distort promotion rates in a way that is tied to the electoral calendar:

> *Secondary observable implication: Democratization amplifies electoral cycles in civil servants' promotions.*

Note that this effect of democratization is relative to the baseline of electoral cycles during autocratic rule. Existing work on budgetary cycles in authoritarian settings suggests that some authoritarian leaders will use the state apparatus to ensure electoral victory not too dissimilar from democracies (see, e.g., Blaydes [2011]; T. Pepinsky [2007]). Authoritarian regimes with no or highly staged and noncompetitive elections have little reason to exert control over their bureaucratic apparatus through the timing of promotions relative to the electoral calendar. In these cases, democratization will induce comparatively strong and new electoral cycles in bureaucratic promotions. In a more competitive electoral authoritarian setting, leaders already rely, to some extent, on promotions during election years to assure effort by their civil servants. Here, democratization may only amplify preexisting promotion cycles. Similar distinctions could be made between national and local elections – the latter being more high-stakes and requiring a more active management by the authoritarian leadership, minimizing the degree of change in the intensity of electoral cycles pre- and post-democratization. The degree of competitiveness in prior authoritarian elections and difference between national and local elections outline important boundary conditions for the amplification effect of democratization for bureaucratic promotion cycles.

The need to exercise bureaucratic control in a democratic setting even extends to democratic elections characterized by programmatic politics. Even

---

[25] See, for example, Chang et al. (2013); Erb & Sulistiyanto (2009); Sumampouw (2016); Warburton (2016).

[26] Theoretical models of electoral cycles differ in their predictions on the exact timing of clientelistic exchanges (Figueroa, 2020; Hanusch & Keefer, 2013; Pierskalla & Sacks, 2020; Toral, 2019). Oliveros (2021), using Argentina as a case study, provides a detailed account of how clientelistic ties can be self-enforcing where civil servants' professional fortunes depend on sustained support from political patrons.

if voters value improved service delivery and public goods, politicians still have incentives to time public expenditures and expansions of visible programs to the electoral cycle (Franzese, 2002; Khemani, 2004; Rogoff, 1990; Saez & Sinha, 2010). This timing effect is likely to be weaker in more programmatic environments, because politicians trying to win elections based on public goods delivery may pursue an alternative strategy of depoliticizing management practices, granting more autonomy, and selecting civil servants with exceptional public sector motivation (Perry & Hondegheim, 2008).[27] While the ad hoc nature of machine politics requires political control, the mass delivery of public goods can be achieved (and improved) by delegating implementation to an autonomous Weberian civil service. This suggests a conceptual boundary condition for my secondary implication. Whereas the *selection-for-competence* effect of democratization is expected to hold across a broad range of cases, the increased demand for political control is likely to be most pronounced in political systems with widespread clientelism. If competitive elections shift the political equilibrium toward a linkage model with programmatic instead of clientelistic parties, we can expect increased legislative oversight and limits to patronage in the bureaucracy (Cruz & Keefer, 2015).[28]

Figure 3 illustrates my theoretical argument. The x-axis represents the extent to which a regime favors personal loyalty over competence in its civil service (arbitrarily scaled from 0 [systems that purely value loyalty] to 1 [those that purely value competence]). The y-axis represents the degree to which the civil service can operate autonomously without the direct intervention of political leaders in everyday management matters (0 = regimes with maximum political control, 1 = those with largely autonomous civil service organizations).

Regimes in Region I are characterized by a strong reliance on personal loyalties. That does not mean that competence plays no role in the selection and promotion of bureaucrats; however, on the margin, such regimes attach a higher premium to personal loyalty. They appoint loyal civil servants and interfere less in the everyday management of the civil service. Individual civil servants may still be reshuffled and sanctioned to minimize the threat to the ruler in cronyist regimes, but this concern is less pressing when high-level bureaucrats were selected based on their loyalty (and comparative incompetence).[29] Few

---

[27] Grzymala-Busse (2007) details how democratization in Eastern Europe has often increased parties' discretionary control of state resources, except where credible opposition parties exert competitive pressure. I instead argue that competitive pressure needs to be paired with a programmatic political environment to generate incentives to depoliticize the civil service.

[28] Reliance on patronage jobs can also decline as a function of intraparty competition (Kemahlioglu, 2011).

[29] Personal networks can also be very effective at screening candidates (Voth & Xu, 2020).

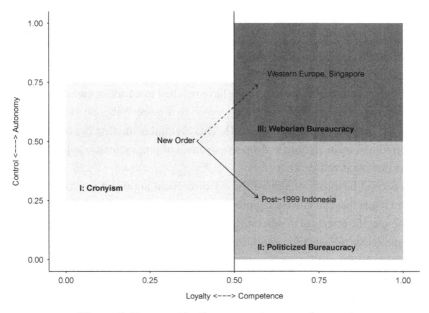

Figure 3 Democratization, competence, and control

regimes are likely to be located in the region closer to the origin on the y-axis for this reason: investing in both strong personal networks to ensure loyalty and a complex machinery to control civil servants with uncertain loyalty is incredibly costly and inefficient. Likewise, moving far away from the origin on the y-axis implies an increasing degree of autonomy within the state bureaucracy, which eventually generates an implicit tension with cronyism due to the need to freely appoint loyal agents regardless of bureaucratic requirements. President Suharto's New Order was a cronyist regime located in Region I (as discussed in the next section).

Democratization, understood as the mere introduction of competitive elections, induces a rightward shift on the x-axis. This represents the *selection-for-competence* effect. It is less clear how it shifts a regime on the y-axis. By default, there is an implied downward shift on the y-axis because an increase in competence implies less emphasis on personal loyalty. Reduced personal loyalty requires a more active effort to control civil servants' behavior to ensure sufficient effort and alignment with the goals of the political leadership. This effect, summarized in the secondary observable implication, is most likely to occur where the political environment favors elections characterized by a lack of programmatic politics. This is the stylized path of the Indonesian civil service after democratization in 1999: an increased emphasis on competence in the civil service emerged in parallel to mass-level clientelism and a politicization of bureaucratic management (a move from Region I to Region II). More generally, this suggests that democratization can have countervailing effects on the state – on the one hand increasing the demand for competence, on the other, amplifying political interference in the everyday management of the civil service. If democratization had happened in a socio-political context that featured programmatic politics, this may have resulted in an additional increase in autonomy on the y-axis, representing a path to a more Weberian bureaucracy (moving from Region I to Region III). This highlights the first boundary condition for the main argument: the pervasiveness of programmatic politics early in the democratization process.

A second boundary condition for my theoretical argument is generated by other factors that can move a regime from Region I to Region III. While I focus on the specific effects of democratization, other factors can also induce changes to a particular bureaucratic equilibrium. In fact, a sizeable literature examines Weberian bureaucracies that have emerged in deeply authoritarian settings. For example, Meiji-era Japan, Taiwan, South Korea, and Singapore were all able to build bureaucracies that emphasize competence paired with a high degree of autonomy, within purely authoritarian settings and without the external pressure of competitive elections (Doner, Ritchie, & Slater, 2005; Evans, 1995). The current literature on the Chinese cadre system similarly emphasizes the dual importance of competence and loyalty within the highly differentiated and complex system of Communist Party rule (Jia, Kudamatsu, & Seim, 2015; Landry, Lü, & Duan, 2018; Shih, Adolph, & Liu, 2012; Xu, 2011). What factors distinguish these cases from the cronyism of Suharto-era Indonesia? Plausible explanations may be tied to the regime's baseline stability in the form of powerful ruling parties or their need to deliver performance to achieve popular legitimacy. As Doner, Ritchie, & Slater (2005) outline, leaders of successful developmental states faced peculiar political environments that threatened their political survival via mass uprisings, paired with a lack of resources to finance patronage-based solutions, which forced them to adopt capable bureaucracies to facilitate economic success. This describes an important set of cases that pursued an alternative pathway from cronyism to competence, which has drawn considerable analytical attention but, as Carothers (2007) points out, is not the norm among authoritarian regimes.

3 Indonesia's Civil Service and the Transition to Democracy

3.1 General Overview and Structure of Indonesia's Civil Service

This section provides a brief, descriptive overview of Indonesia's civil service history, structure, and general changes since democratization in 1999 before the detailed analysis of democratization's effect on management practices in

Section 4. Both sections analyze a variety of material, but uniquely draw on a novel source of micro-level data on Indonesia's bureaucracy: the BKN Civil Servant Database. This database was created in collaboration with Indonesia's civil service agency (BKN, *Badan Kepegawaian Negara*) and the World Bank's Jakarta office. It contains information on all of the country's four + million civil servants who were active in 2015.[30] The database includes an individual entry for each civil servant, which details basic characteristics such as gender, age, religion, educational attainment, place of birth, current workplace, job type, civil service rank, and date of entry into the civil service.[31] The cross section provides a detailed and comprehensive overview of Indonesia's civil service that I leverage to assess its current state and evolution since democratization in 1999. Given the paucity of comprehensive, micro-level data on civil service organizations in either the developed or developing world, these data offer an important opportunity for quantitative research on the civil service.

Indonesia's civil service has its origins in a system of courtiers from the Javanese aristocracy (*priyayi*) and the Dutch colonial administration. The Dutch system of indirect colonial rule employed the indigenous aristocracy as intermediaries, who were selected via hereditary succession rather than merit, merging the administrative layer of the colonial state with the preexisting social strata of traditional leaders (Quah, 2016; Vickers, 2005). This created a hybrid between a traditional patrimonial bureaucracy and a Western, Weberian version of the state apparatus (Evers, 1987). Like many colonial bureaucracies, it was small (around 100,000 individuals at the height of the colonial period) and had a limited geographic reach. The highest echelons were typically occupied by Dutch citizens (Bachtiar, 1972). The Dutch colonial bureaucracy was focused on colonial rule and extraction, leaving little positive legacy for effective public government (Pramusinto, 2016; Quah, 2016).

After independence in 1945, the Indonesian government, pursuing an explicit strategy of state-building and rejecting the legacy of colonial rule, created a unitary government structure. The new civil service replaced the indigenous aristocracy as an extension of the colonial state with a new class of nationalist activists who had fought for independence. This led to the first drastic expansion of the civil service, which gave political parties enormous influence over the appointment of civil servants (Feith, 1962), leading to the creation of a bloated and ineffective civil service (Vickers, 2005, pp. 124–125).

---

[30] The database excludes retired employees, military personnel, police officers, and members of BIN, Indonesia's state intelligence agency.

[31] It does not include their salaries, but remuneration is determined according to rank, job assignment, and age.

From 1965 to 1998, Indonesia was governed by a starkly centralized authoritarian regime under the leadership of General Suharto. After taking power in the wake of a purported coup attempt (Roosa, 2006), Suharto consolidated his power quickly and engaged in an anti-communist campaign of mass murder. Having eliminated the Indonesian Communist Party as a political force, his *Orde Baru* (New Order) regime centralized decision-making power around the presidency and ruled the country with the help of the military, the ruling party Golkar (*Golongan Karya*, which translates as "functional groups"), and the civil service (Liddle, 1985). The latter two were intimately intertwined (Emmerson, 1983). The Golkar party started as an association of functional groups, one of which was of civil servants. Golkar became a political vehicle for the regime and a highly effective tool for winning authoritarian elections. All civil servants were required to support Golkar; they constituted a core pillar of support for the regime (Mietzner, 2018a). Suharto also made sure that civil servants were loyal to him and Golkar and not any other political force, severing any link between independence-era political parties and the civil service (Logsdon, 1992; Warwick, 1987). Law 8/1974 placed all civil servants under strict central government control and cemented the state bureaucracy's status as a pillar of the regime. Windfall revenue from oil and gas also allowed President Suharto to engage in a number of large government projects in the 1970s, including a substantial expansion of the civil service (Evers, 1987). In turn, becoming a civil servant and willing participant in Suharto's rule came with substantial economic and social privileges.[32] While in the pyramidal structure of the regime, the presidency was centered at the top, followed by the military, the larger bureaucracy exerted a powerful role for regime survival, due to its deep penetration of society and control over policy decision-making (Liddle, 1985).

The Suharto regime is considered a hybrid case of authoritarian rule: featuring elements of military rule, relying on a dominant ruling party to win authoritarian elections, and, over time, becoming increasingly personalist in character. In terms of solving the problem of authoritarian control (Svolik, 2012), that is, containing threats by the masses, the regime relied on the repressive power of the military, a skillful sidelining of opposition forces through a combination of cooptation and repression (Aspinall, 2005), and the delivery of impressive rates of economic development (Liddle, 1985). How did Suharto manage his elite coalition, that is, "authoritarian power-sharing" (Svolik, 2012)? Early on, Suharto relied on military officers in his cabinet, high-level ministerial,

---

[32] For example, a regular allotments of subsidized rice and access to better schooling (Liddle, 1987).

and political positions to maintain control. By relying on trusted confederates with a shared history in the armed forces, Suharto was able to establish a tight grip over state institutions. The military's dual role (*dwifungsi*) in military and civilian affairs, controlling key bureaucratic, political, and economic positions, provided the president a powerful tool for sidelining rivaling elite factions. Initial military dominance subsequently gave way to "bureaucratic pluralism" (Emmerson, 1983), partially diluting military control with civilian fiefdoms, and, eventually, increasingly personalist rule by Suharto in the late phase of the regime (McIntyre, 2005; Vatikiotis, 1998). Even when relying on the support of fellow military officers, Suharto was keenly aware of his personal relationships with specific individuals and did not blindly trust the military as an institution (Vatikiotis, 1998, p. 75). He used his ability to reassign and shuffle individuals across positions of power to foster factionalism within the military and with other elite groups (Pepinsky, 2009, Ch. 3).

Another key element in maintaining the stability of the ruling coalition was the delivery of private rents. The heavily centralized system of autocratic rule, centered around Suharto and his immediate circle of cronies, provided access to positions that allowed the abuse of state power for private gain (McLeod, 2008). By forging alliances with wealthy business tycoons, allowing military officers to engage in off-budget business endeavors, and facilitating the theft of state resources, Suharto was able to deliver substantial rents to his supporters. Clientelism and patronage were widely used to sustain regime support, providing the mortar to hold the different parts of the regime together (Crouch, 1979; McLeod, 2000). By carefully selecting and placing personal cronies into positions of power, making access to lucrative rents conditional on personal approval, and sidelining actors that amassed too much independent power, Suharto was able to remain in office despite having to weather multiple economic and political crises (McIntyre, 2005; Vatikiotis, 1998). The internal regime dynamics of the New Order regime vividly illustrate the political utility of cronyism and the dangers of competence for authoritarian survival (Zakharov, 2016).

The increasingly personalist and cronyist nature of the regime also trickled down into the lower levels of the state's machinery (Mackie, 2010). Civil service promotions clearly prioritized rent seeking, political patronage, and maintaining regime stability over merit (McLeod, 2008). Personal connections and patronage were the organizing principles of the civil service (McVey, 1982). Shrewdly, Suharto set official salaries for civil servants low enough to make them dependent on discretionary benefits allocated by superiors and lucrative, extralegal rent-seeking opportunities, tying their economic fortunes to Suharto's approval (Mackie, 2010). However, the New Order regime did not completely disregard considerations of technical proficiency in the civil service. Logsdon (1992) documents a decrease in the number of illiterate civil servants in the 1970s as a consequence of stricter standards and general educational advances in Indonesia. At the top of the civil service, foreign-educated technocrats (known as the "Berkeley Mafia") played an important role in economic policy-making, especially during crises and when dealing with international financial institutions, but these employees had no permanent or deep political backing within the regime (Datta et al., 2011).

How then did this remarkably resilient regime fall? In 1999, the East Asian Financial Crisis triggered an unexpected and sudden transition to democracy (Crouch, 2010). The massive shock to the financial system ruptured the elite coalition that supported Suharto (T. B. Pepinsky, 2007). Faced with popular protests in the streets, mounting international pressure, and capital flight by powerful economic elites, he was forced to step down and make way for reforms. The country held national and local elections in 1999 and passed a massive decentralization reform (Crouch, 2010).[33]

Indonesia's current democratic government is organized in three layers: the central government, provincial governments (*pemerintah provinsi*), and district-level governments (*pemerintah kabupaten* and *kota*). The decentralization reforms sidelined provinces by delegating essential government responsibilities, such as health care and education, to the district level. Responsibility for local public goods provision is paired with a complex system of revenue-sharing and regional redistribution (World Bank, 2003). District government revenue comes from shared revenue allocations and block grants from the central government. Local taxation authority remains fairly limited: districts have to rely on special fees and licenses to generate their own revenue (Lewis, 2005). To help districts shoulder these new responsibilities, over two million civil servants, particularly teachers and health-care workers, were reassigned to district governments, which reduced the control of national ministries and agencies. As of 2018, less than one million civil servants (22.44 percent) were employed by central government institutions; the remaining 3.2 million work for provincial and district governments.[34]

National elections have been fairly free and competitive, albeit marred by occasional violence and a lack of programmatic politics (Crouch, 2010). Vote buying and mass-level clientelism have been on the rise (Aspinall &

---

[33] Laws No. 22/1999, No. 25/1999, and No. 32/2004 specify the key elements of Indonesia's decentralization. Law No. 23/2014 clarified and updated earlier reforms.

[34] This split between national and subnational government employees has been roughly stable since the initial decentralization reforms.

Berenschot, 2019), as have anti-democratic, populist, and exclusionary attitudes at the mass and elite levels across the political spectrum (Aspinall et al., 2019; Aspinall & Mietzner, 2019; Buehler, 2016; Mietzner, 2014, 2015). Since the decentralization reforms, local political authority has been shared between the office of the district head (*bupati* or *walikota*) and the local legislature. Together, they have the authority to pass local budgets and vote on local laws and regulations, although district heads have greater authority than the legislature to set the agenda.

At first, district heads were indirectly elected; candidates had to acquire a majority of votes in the local legislature to be appointed. They had to be nominated by parties (or coalitions of parties) represented in the local parliament, which often led to the selling of party nominations and votes to rich local candidates (Buehler, 2010). District heads have been directly elected since 2005 in an effort to dispel the appearance of elite collusion and enhance transparency and accountability (Erb & Sulistiyanto, 2009). While candidates are still required to secure party nominations,[35] bargaining in the legislature has been replaced by competitive general voting. This institutional change has created a competitive (albeit still elite-dominated) local electoral process (Erb & Sulistiyanto, 2009). The decentralization reforms also allowed government units to be split, and new district governments to be created. This process of district proliferation has dramatically increased the number of local governments and generated new challenges for organizing local civil service units and hiring new staff (Lewis, 2017; Pierskalla, 2016).

Indonesia's civil service has increased from around 3.6 million employees in 2006 to over four million (roughly 1.6 percent of the current population); personnel expenditures account for roughly a quarter of total state revenue (Tjiptoherijanto, 2007).[36] Its overall size is comparable to the bureaucracies of other countries in the region (Tjiptoherijanto, 2007), but, relative to the size of the workforce, is below average compared to the Organisation for Economic Cooperation and Development and other Southeast Asian nations (OECD & Asian Development Bank, 2019, p. 57).

Civil servants are employed by over 600 distinct government units, including regional and local governments, and thirty-two national ministries and

---

[35] Independent candidates are allowed, but the regulatory and financial burden is considered prohibitively high.

[36] After years of continuous (albeit slow) growth, the overall number of civil servants declined from 2009 to 2018 due to increasing waves of retirements, paired with strict quotas on the intake of new civil servants and a five-year moratorium on hiring that was announced by the Widodo government in 2014.

agencies.[37] Figures 4 and 5 display the total number of civil servants and the number of civil servants relative to the local population for each district government, respectively. Both figures illustrate the substantial subnational variation in state presence, as measured by the number of civil servants.

Approximately 54 percent of the country's total population (147 million people) live on the island of Java, which has the largest provincial and district governments. The provinces of Central Java, East Java, and West Java have the highest absolute number of civil servants – each has over 300,000 employees. Other islands, such as Papua, have a higher density of civil servants. Given Indonesia's size, varied geography, population distribution, and highly diverse citizenry, its administrative penetration varies greatly throughout the country.

The civil service as a whole operates under the supervision and guidance of three national departments and agencies: the state Ministry for Administrative Reforms (MenPAN, *Menteri Negara Pendayagunaan Aparatur Negara*), the National Institute of Public Administration (LAN, *Lembaga Administrasi Negara*), and the BKN. The 2014 Civil Service Reform Law[38] also created a Civil Service Commission, consisting of seven members from government, academia, and civil society, to oversee the implementation of the public sector ethics code. While these national-level oversight institutions have some control over the general operation of the civil service – such as payroll, performance appraisals, and staffing – they share management responsibilities with line ministries and regional and local governments (OECD & Asian Development Bank, 2019, p. 77). Provincial and district governments enjoy substantial latitude in the practical, everyday management of civil servants.

Civil service positions are highly competitive; job openings have historically been oversubscribed. The civil service is a very popular career path for college students (Banuri & Keefer, 2016). The selection process consists of several stages. Applicants are prescreened based on their educational attainment and prior work experience, and must pass a written exam that assesses their general competency, personality, and national loyalty. Cheating, leveraging familial connections, bribery, and scams are common practices to secure coveted public sector positions (Blunt, Turner, & Lindroth, 2012a, 2012b; Kristiansen & Ramli, 2006; Tidey, 2012). In 2013, a new computer-assisted entrance exam was piloted to combat some of these issues.[39]

---

[37] National ministries vary dramatically in size. The largest ones – the Ministry of Religion and the Ministry for Education, Culture, and Research, Technology – employ over 100,000 civil servants, whereas the smallest have fewer than 100 employees.

[38] Law No. 5/2014.

[39] While not introduced uniformly at first, early impressions were positive, suggesting the new process was more transparent and credible (Beschel et al., 2018). In 2014, the government

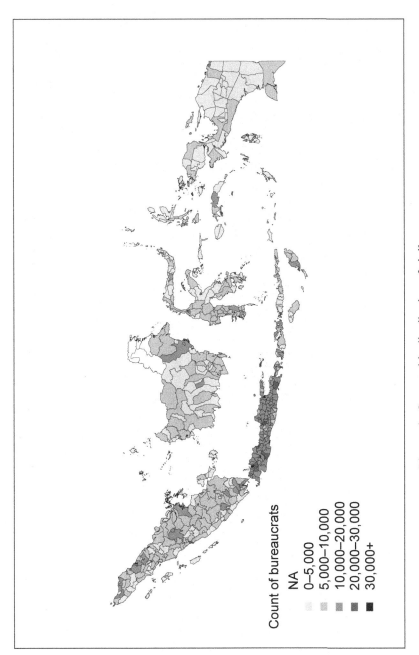

Figure 4 Geographic distribution of civil servants

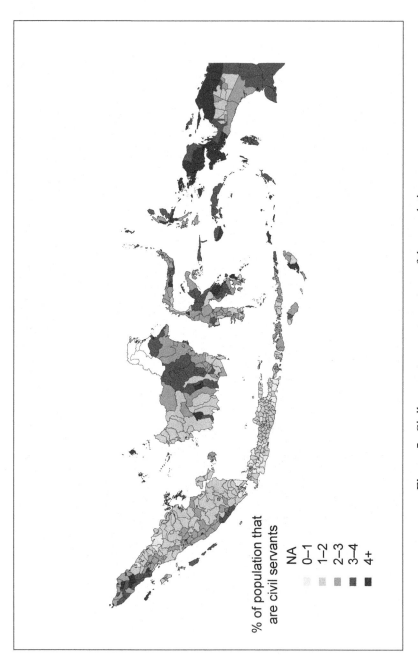

Figure 5 Civil servants as a percentage of the population

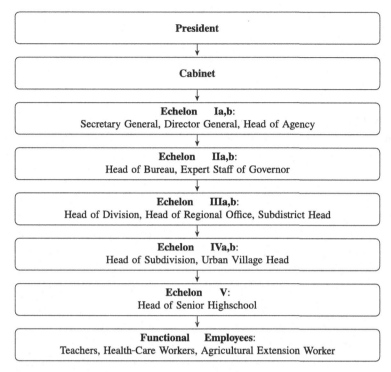

Figure 6 The echelon hierarchy

Civil servants are broadly classified into three categories: functional (general), and functional (special), and structural. Functional employees mostly consist of frontline civil servants including teachers and health-care workers, who compromise the bulk of all civil servants (89 percent). Structural employees typically have managerial responsibilities and rank higher in the hierarchy.

The hierarchy of the civil service is structured based on so-called echelon ranks (see Figure 6).[40] This echelon structure has remained consistent throughout the Suharto regime and the post-1999 democratic period. All civil servants initially enter without an echelon rank. Advancing on the echelon scale requires merit-based promotions, which confer higher status, authority, salary,[41] and

---

switched to the new computer-assisted test, but actual use has been lagging, in part due to the five-year moratorium on hiring (2014–2019).

[40] The parallel four-level *golongan* classification scheme is an alternative hierarchy. Advancement is largely a function of educational attainment and age. *Golongan* does not directly indicate hierarchical career progression in the civil service, since even teachers, who are typically below the echelon classification, can attain the highest level. However, a minimum *golongan* is necessary to advance on the echelon scale.

[41] Civil servants' salaries are determined by strict schedules that take into account the level of responsibility, local cost of living, and job type. A number of official and unofficial allowances

Political Economy

Table 1 Number of civil servants across echelon ranks

Echelon rank	Men	%	Women	%	Total	%
Echelon I	735	0.16	233	0.05	968	0.21
Echelon II	19,167	4.15	3,358	0.73	22,525	4.88
Echelon III	77,427	16.78	23,349	5.06	100,776	21.84
Echelon IV	212,295	46.00	124,922	27.07	337,217	73.07
Total	309,624	67.09	151,862	32.91	461,486	100

managerial responsibility. Echelon ranks range from level IV to the top levels of Ia and Ib.[42] At the district government level, a typical echelon IV civil servant would be the head of a subdivision (*kecamatan*) or a technical implementation unit. At the national level, echelon IV employees are heads of sections. At the top of the hierarchy, ranks Ia and Ib include directors general, deputy cabinet secretaries, and agency heads.[43]

Promotions require meeting certain minimum criteria related to work experience, favorable performance reviews,[44] and a recommendation from the employee's promotion panel. Promotion panels consist of superior officers and are required to evaluate candidates for higher-level positions based on meritocratic principles. More often than not, promotion decisions are politicized, especially at the district level, where elected mayors have substantial control over personnel decisions (Berenschot, 2018a).

Table 1 shows the breakdown of civil servants across the broad echelon ranks. The vast majority (73 percent) of echelon-level civil servants are employed at level IV; only about 5 percent attain the rank of level I or II. Across echelon ranks, there exists an obvious gender disparity. Women make up only 33 percent of all echelon-level employees. At the top level (echelon I), there are more than three times as many men. At echelon II, there are nearly six

---

and nonpecuniary benefits supplement their basic salary (e.g., special allotments of rice, holiday bonuses). Drawing on representative labor market surveys across several countries, Finan, Olken, & Pande (2015) document that Indonesian civil servants as a whole enjoy a substantial wage premium over the private sector. At higher levels of the bureaucratic hierarchy, compensation is low compared to the private sector (Tjiptoherijanto, 2014).

[42] Echelon level V is deprecated since Indonesia's Law No. 5 Year 2014 on the Civil Service Apparatus. Nonetheless, civil servants of that echelon level are still actively employed.

[43] The highest rank that civil servants employed by Indonesia's district governments (the third, but functionally important, level of government) can attain is IIa.

[44] Nuswantoro (2017) details how performance reviews in the past relied on vague and subjective criteria, and maintains that recent reforms have not drastically improved this aspect of career advancement.

times as many men as women. Pierskalla and colleagues (2021) document how democratization has amplified the career penalty for female civil servants.

The post-democratization civil service reforms have only slowly impacted the operation of Indonesia's bureaucracy. Reform law No. 43/1999 allowed for increased flexibility to supplement civil servant salaries, depending on the local cost of living, and codified a merit-based personnel management approach. In 2014, the ambitious Law No. 5/2014 introduced strong formal principles of meritocracy, codifying competitive recruitment to high-level positions and explicitly outlawing discrimination based on gender, religion, or political affiliation. Despite these new regulatory mandates, substantive progress has been minimal. Across central and regional government units, higher-level positions are often awarded without proper competitive selection procedures, and the outright buying and selling of civil service positions remains pervasive (Blunt, Turner, & Lindroth, 2012b; Kristiansen & Ramli, 2006; Suwitri, Supriyono, & Kuswandaru, 2019). A member of the national Civil Service Commission estimates that 90 percent of civil service organizations are involved in the practice of buying and selling of positions, and identified the Ministries of Education, Health, and Religion as particularly affected (Suwitri, Supriyono, & Kuswandaru, 2019).

While general progress toward meritocracy has been slow, there have been pockets of successful reform, such as in the Ministry of Finance. After 1999, the ministry struggled to recruit high-quality candidates due to the comparatively low pay, inefficient internal organizations, poor management, and widespread corruption (LaForge, 2016). Finance Minister Sri Mulyani Indrawati, in her first stint in the position from 2005 to 2010, implemented substantial and meaningful changes. She clarified portfolios and management responsibilities, pushed out problematic, high-level civil servants, and introduced pay supplements to bolster recruitment efforts, despite resistance from a variety of stakeholders.

3.2 Competence and Skills

Before providing an in-depth analysis of the relationship between democratization and competence in Section 4, this section briefly describes the key demographic features of Indonesia's civil servants.

The country's civil service – especially at the top levels – has traditionally been dominated by fairly educated Muslim men, often from the main island of Java. Table 1 demonstrated the dominance of male civil servants in leadership positions. Women are much better represented in functional roles: they comprise 51 percent of nonechelon employees. The proportion of religious minorities (i.e., non-Muslims) in the civil service matches the general population shares (see Table 2). Figure 7 demonstrates the dominance of Java-born civil servants, followed by those from North Sumatra and South Sulawesi.

Civil servants' educational attainment ranges broadly (Figure 8). The Indonesian educational system covers primary school (*Sekolah Dasar*, SD), junior high school (*Sekolah Menengah Pertama*, SMP), high school (*Sekolah Menengah Atas*, SMA), followed by college. College education can be distinguished between one to three years of college, a completed undergraduate degree (*Sarjana Strata 1*, S1), a master's degree (*Sarjana Strata Dua*, S2), and a doctorate degree (*Sarjana Strata 3*, S3).

As of 2018, the level of education of Indonesian civil servants ranges from elementary school level (SD) to graduate-level university degrees (S2/S3). More than 50 percent have finished a four-year university degree, but a surprisingly large number (21 percent) have only a high school education. More than 75 percent of all civil servants have some level of college education: 52 percent have completed a four-year Bachelor's degree, and just under 10 percent (9.55 percent) have completed postgraduate studies.

To calculate educational attainment across groups or geographic units, I construct a simple ordinal variable (1 = SD, 2 = SMP, 3 = SMA, 4 = Diploma 1-3, 5 = Diploma 4/S1, and 6 = S2/S3). Figure 9 shows the average level of educational attainment across district governments. Unsurprisingly, there is substantial geographic variation in average competency across local government units: average education ranges from 3.54 in Kabupaten Malaka to 4.74 in Kota Serang.[45] The province with the highest educational attainment among civil servants is Banten (4.9); the lowest is Papua (4.17). Regions close to Jakarta and on Java show the highest levels of education attainment. On average, employees of provincial and district governments have lower educational attainment than those who work for the central government.

Across the echelon hierarchy of the civil service, average educational attainment increases with rank: top-level officials, on average, have advanced degrees (see Table 3).

There are pronounced differences across central government ministries and agencies; the average educational attainment ranges from 2.98 to 5.36. The ministries with the most highly educated civil servants include the Audit Board of the Republic of Indonesia; the Ministry for Research, Technology, and Higher Education; and the Ministry of Home Affairs. Those with the lowest average educational attainment are the State Police, the Ministry of Defense

---

[45] Spatial disparities are even greater for technical job categories such as medical services (Asian Development Bank, 2021).

Table 2 Gender and religious affiliation across echelon levels

Echelon	% Female	% Muslim	% Catholic	% Protestant	% Hindu	% Buddhist	% Confucian	% Other
Echelon 1	0.276	0.888	0.032	0.067	0.013	0	0	0
Echelon 2	0.163	0.792	0.047	0.140	0.021	>0	0	0
Echelon 3	0.215	0.791	0.048	0.141	0.019	0.001	0	>0
Echelon 4	0.351	0.815	0.043	0.123	0.019	>0	>0	>0
Nonechelon	0.515	0.825	0.041	0.110	0.024	>0	>0	>0
General population	0.497	0.870	0.030	0.070	0.017	0.007	0.005	0.001

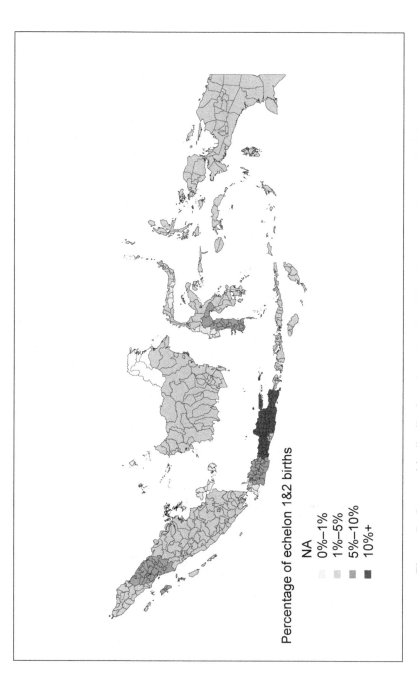

Percentage of echelon 1&2 births

NA
0%–1%
1%–5%
5%–10%
10%+

Figure 7 Geographic distribution of echelon 1 and 2 civil servants, by area of origin

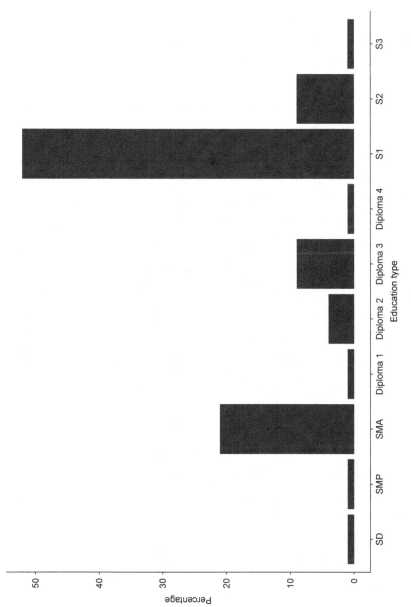

Figure 8 Civil servants' educational attainment

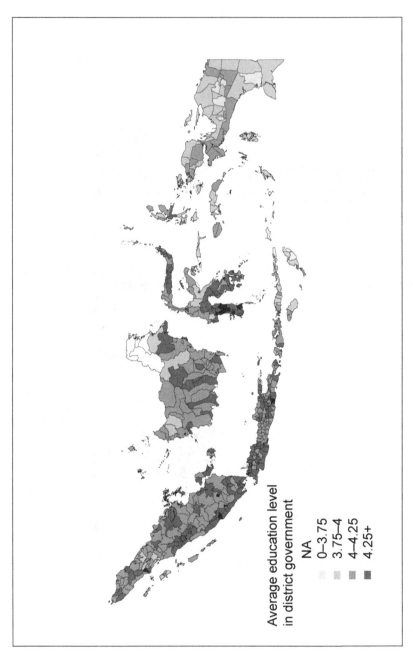

Figure 9 Geographic distribution of civil servants' average education level

Table 3 Average education across echelon levels

Echelon	Avg Edu
Echelon I	5.71
Echelon II	5.76
Echelon III	5.65
Echelon IV, V	4.63
All civil servants	3.60

(civilian administrators only), and the Ministry of Transportation. Units dealing with complex technical topics tend to employ more highly educated civil servants.

Beyond general educational attainment, civil servants in Indonesia are also required to complete a number of on-the-job training programs throughout their career, covering topics like management techniques, project management skills, digital competency, and specific technical expertise (Tjiptoherijanto, 2018).[46]

While the main focus of the subsequent analysis is the role of educational attainment as a proxy for civil servant competence, one other measure of competence is worth exploring for descriptive purposes. To comply with the mandate in the civil service reform law of 2014 to create a more explicit performance metric for civil service organizations, the BKN developed the Professionalism Index (PI) to measure the overall "professionalism" of civil service units. The index has four core inputs: *qualification, competence, discipline,* and *performance.* Civil servants' *qualification* is operationalized via educational attainment. *Competence* is measured as the completion rate of required training workshops. *Discipline* is scored based on the number of disciplinary infractions in the official administrative records. *Performance* is quantified via official performance reviews conducted by superiors. The four dimensions are combined into a final index, weighted at 25%, 40%, 30%, and 5%, respectively. The total scores range from <60 ("very low professionalism"), 61–70 ("low professionalism"), 71–80 ("moderate professionalism"), 81–90 ("high professionalism"), to 91–100 ("very high professionalism"). BKN surveyed 1,525,822 civil servants (36.6 percent of all civil servants) for the initial PI data collection. Response rates varied substantially across civil service units, from close to zero in the Ministry of Rural, Rural Development and

---

[46] See Asian Development Bank (2021) for a more detailed breakdown.

Transmigration to 100 percent for the Ministry of Home Affairs. As it is unclear whether BKN used a random-sampling procedure in its data collection, I cannot be certain that the PI score is representative of the entire Indonesian civil service (or of specific organizations) because reporting is likely to be correlated with underlying levels of professionalism. Nor has the index been validated or tested for reliability.[47]

With these caveats in mind, the PI reveals substantial variation within the civil service. The average score across all civil service organizations is 68.5 (out of 100) for central government units and 62.7 for regional government units – a low level of professionalism according to BKN's classification. Top central government units are the Coordinating Ministry for Maritime Affairs and Investment with a score of eighty-two and the Coordinating Ministry of Human Development and Culture with a score of eighty-five. The worst performers are the Ministry of Youth and Sports (PI = 56), the Ministry of Environment and Forests (PI = 56), and the Ministry of Law and Human Rights (PI = 52). Figure 10 maps the variation in PI scores across district governments.

These descriptive patterns generate a decidedly mixed picture of Indonesia's civil service. On the one hand, its formal bureaucratic structures and procedures adhere to the general outlines of the Weberian ideal. Since democratization in 1999, formal rules and regulations have enshrined the principles of meritocracy and impartiality in the civil service. Yet on the other hand, the practical operation is quite different. While competence is relevant in civil servants' selection and promotion, there are numerous indications that the Indonesian civil service is plagued by corruption, clientelism, and increased politicization. In the next section, I investigate the extent to which democratization has changed management practices in the civil service.

4 Democratization, Competence, and Control

To assess how democratization has influenced the importance placed on civil servants' competence in promotion decisions, I leverage the detailed quantitative records contained the BKN civil servant database. I supplement basic cross-sectional demographic information on all civil servants in 2015 with details of each individual's past job assignments – including the workplace, work location, job type, and associated rank – to construct a panel data set with the civil-servant-year as the unit of analysis. Observations begin when the employees entered the civil service and end in 2015.[48] For example, a teacher

---

[47] I use variation in the response rate as a measure of civil service capacity in Section 4.

[48] I restrict the analysis to civil-servant-years after 1980 to exclude the small number of individuals who served longer than the mandatory retirement age allows.

Figure 10 Professionalism index across district governments

who started in 1980 would generate a total of thirty-six civil-servant-year observations. Since the vast majority of civil servants spend their entire thirty to forty
year career in government service, the data cover a large portion of individuals
who have been active since the early 1990s. Reconstructing career trajectories
that span the 1980–2015 time period allows me to observe the returns to competence with respect to advancing through the echelon ranks of Indonesia's civil
service.

4.1 Measurement and Variable Definitions

To measure career progression in Indonesia's civil service, I rely on the official *echelon* classification system, which indicates the level of hierarchy a
management-level civil servant has attained (see Figure 6). I use this system
to generate a binary variable that captures a promotion event in any given
civil-servant-year.[49] Promotions are a useful outcome measure for at least
two reasons. First, they are one of the most important rewards and signifiers
of career progression in hierarchical bureaucratic systems, and affect civil
servant effort and engagement (Bertrand et al., 2020; Karachiwalla & Park,
2017). If democratization has a *selection-for-competence* effect, this should be
reflected in decisions about career advancement on the echelon scale. Second,
promotions capture the practical application (or lack thereof) of meritocratic
principles. While changes to laws and regulations governing the civil service
are an important alternative metric of meritocracy, they can be misleading. Formal institutional changes are neither necessary nor sufficient for the application
of merit in practice (Schuster, 2017); in low-income countries they often reflect
"isomorphic mimicry" – that is, the ineffectual aping of advanced industrialized
countries' institutions (Andrews, Pritchett, & Woolcock, 2017).

To capture the extent to which competence is valued under autocracy and
democracy, I use educational attainment as a proxy. To measure educational
attainment, I create a variable that can take six distinct categorical outcomes: elementary school (reference category), junior high school, senior high
school, diploma I/II/III (equivalent to one to three years of college), diploma
IV/bachelor (four years of college), and postgraduate degree.

While not a perfect proxy for civil servants' quality, skill, or ability, a large
literature on human capital in economics has argued that education predicts
earnings, which indicates that it proxies for skill – or at least the ability to *signal*
one's skill level (Card, 1999). Educational attainment has also been widely used

---

[49] The variable captures any upward movement on the echelon scale, starting with the initial
promotion of *functional employees*, which lack an echelon rank, to the category of *structural*
employees with some management responsibility.

in the study of political selection and the quality of political candidates (Besley & Reynal-Querol, 2011; Ferraz & Finan, 2011). Some empirical work has also documented a link between educational attainment and improved governance. For example, the massive expansion of schooling in Indonesia in the 1970s has been found to have increased both the educational attainment of candidates for public office and the quality of public goods provision (Martinez-Bravo, 2017). Similarly, work on Chinese bureaucrats has found that educated civil servants perform better at poverty alleviation (He & Wang, 2017).

In the models without individual-level fixed effects, I include additional covariates that are important predictors of career advancement and might correlate with educational attainment – gender, religious affiliation, age, and total years of work experience. Gender is a simple binary variable that takes a value of 1 for individuals identified as female in the database (0 otherwise), while religious affiliation is captured in seven distinct categories: Muslim (reference category), Protestant, Catholic, Hindu, Buddhist, Confucian, and Other. A civil servant's age and total years of work experience in the civil service are simple count variables.

4.2 Research Design

The data allow me to observe individual career trajectories before and after Indonesia's sudden democratization in 1999, which was triggered by the Asian Financial Crisis (Crouch, 2010; Pepinsky, 2009). While rumors before this time hinted that Suharto was in poor health and was unlikely to remain in office much longer (Fisman, 2001), neither the eventual timing of his departure nor the regime's transition to democracy was widely expected. The president and his ruling Golkar party had garnered 74.51 percent of the popular vote and 76.47 percent of seats in the legislature in the 1997 elections, which suggests the regime was still strong at that point.

I exploit this sudden, unplanned transition for identification purposes. Since Suharto's ruling coalition did not anticipate his downfall or an imminent transition to democracy, promotion patterns in the civil service before 1999 very likely followed an established logic that supported the regime's needs. After 1999, the shift toward democratic elections placed elected politicians in control of the civil service, which might have led to a change in promotion practices. Note that Indonesia serves as a hard test of my theoretical expectations since nearly all of the elites in the military, civil service, and ruling party retained their positions, which makes it less likely that I will observe any sudden shifts in regime behavior.

I estimate the effects of democratization in a difference-in-differences setting:

$$y_{idpgt} = \alpha_i + \gamma_d + \eta_p + \rho_g + \tau_t + \beta \cdot \text{Edu}_{it} + \delta \cdot \text{post-1999}_t \cdot \text{Edu}_{it} + \theta \cdot \mathbf{z}_{it} + \epsilon_{idpgt}$$

Where y_{idpgt} is a binary dependent variable indicating a promotion event in year t, α_i is an individual-level fixed effect, γ_d is a civil service department fixed effect, η_p is a province-of-birth fixed effect, ρ_g is a *rank* fixed effect, and τ_t is a year fixed effect. My analyses include year effects to model secular changes in promotion patterns and varying combinations of group fixed effects. In the most lenient specification, I combine department and province-of-birth effects, which allows us to estimate the baseline effect of educational attainment edu_{it} and additional individual-level controls $\mathbf{z}_{it}$ such as gender, and religion, age, and work experience. In the most conservative specification, I include the more general individual-level fixed effects, which absorb the individual-level covariates and province-of-birth fixed effects. To capture the effects of democratization, I include an interaction term of a post-1999 dummy variable with educational attainment. The constituent term for the post-democratization dummy is always absorbed in the year fixed effects. The coefficient δ is the main effect of interest, because it captures the extent to which democratization has changed the effect of educational attainment.

The fixed effects cover the individual's province of birth, to account for the influence of cultural and ethnic networks in the civil service, and department unit fixed effects. The latter control for unobserved confounders at the unit level to account for the fact that some departments, such as the central bank, might have specific educational requirements or be governed by department-specific norms. Last, some of the model specifications include fixed effects to indicate an individual's *golongan* or rank.

Overall, causal identification is plausible in this case because the exogenous nature of the democratization reform, paired with a battery of fixed effects, ought to render the influence of unobservable characteristics negligible. I use this difference-in-differences setting to estimate the variation in the promotion premiums associated with different levels of educational attainment. The underlying parallel-trends assumption is that in the absence of democratization, promotion patterns across educational categories would have evolved in parallel. Appendix B discusses this assumption in more detail.

One concern may be that democratization changed the civil service recruitment patterns. For example, more regime-critical individuals might have opted to enter the civil service after 1999, which could have changed the composition of civil servants in terms of either observable or unobservable characteristics. Comparing the demographic profiles of incoming cohorts (see Appendix C), I find very few differences around the year of democratization (1994–2004). More generally, the civil service as a career choice has been continuously popular in Indonesia (Banuri & Keefer, 2015), making deep compositional shifts in the applicant pool unlikely. To further safeguard against this concern, I also analyze a subsample of the data that only includes individuals hired before 1999. These individuals were subject to the same recruitment process under autocratic rule. For this set of observations, I can compare an individual's chances of promotion before versus after 1999. I estimate these models using a standard ordinary least squares (OLS) method and cluster standard errors at the individual level.

4.3 Main Results: *Selection-for-Competence*

I begin by assessing changes in the effect of educational attainment on promotions. Table 4 displays the coefficient estimates for a variety of models. Model (1) is the lenient specification with individual-level covariates, province of birth, department, and year fixed effects. Model (2) replaces province of birth with individual-level fixed effects, and Model (3) adds *golongan* fixed effects. Models (4)–(6) have the same specification, but use the subsample of civil servants hired before 1999. Starting with Model (1), the table shows that educational attainment has a positive and statistically significant (below the 1 percent level) effect on promotions before 1999. For example, civil servants who acquired a postgraduate degree are 4 percentage points more likely to be promoted in any given year (the unconditional probability of promotion in the sample is only 1.5 percent). Clearly, although loyalty may matter to autocratic rulers, competence was still rewarded in Indonesia's civil service before 1999. It is noteworthy that the baseline effect size before democratization increases in educational attainment, that is, higher levels of educational attainment have larger effects, as one would expect if educational attainment proxies for competence.

The interaction terms in Model (1) indicate that the premium for educational attainment increased after 1999, especially for the highest levels of education. In effect, the same civil servant with a postgraduate education experienced an additional 3-percentage-point increase in the probability of being promoted after 1999 versus before the transition. The same is true for nearly all categories of educational attainment above elementary schooling.

Models (2) and (3) provide additional evidence of this shift in the value of education in promotion decisions. While these models do not allow me to identify the baseline premium for educational attainment before 1999, I can still estimate the differential change after democratization. In both models, I find clear evidence that the premium for education increased under democracy. Models (4)–(6) provide further support for this pattern. Even when I restrict

Table 4 Promotion analysis: Education

	Promotion	Promotion	Promotion	Promotion	Promotion	Promotion
	(1)	(2)	(3)	(4)	(5)	(6)
Education: Junior High	0.003*** (0.0004)			0.002*** (0.0004)		
Education: Senior High	0.01*** (0.0002)			0.004*** (0.0002)		
Education: Diploma I/II/III	0.01*** (0.0002)			0.005*** (0.0002)		
Education: Diploma IV/S1	0.01*** (0.0002)			0.01*** (0.0002)		
Education: Post-graduate	0.04*** (0.0005)			0.03*** (0.001)		

	(1)	(2)	(3)	(4)	(5)	(6)
Education: Junior High × Post-democratization	0.0003	0.001***	0.001***	0.002***	0.001***	0.001***
	(0.0003)	(0.0003)	(0.0003)	(0.0003)	(0.0003)	(0.0003)
Education: Senior High × Post-democratization	0.01***	0.01***	0.01***	0.01***	0.01***	0.01***
	(0.0002)	(0.0002)	(0.0002)	(0.0002)	(0.0002)	(0.0002)
Education: Diploma I/II/III × Post-democratization	0.01***	0.002***	0.002***	0.002***	0.002***	0.002***
	(0.0002)	(0.0001)	(0.0001)	(0.0002)	(0.0001)	(0.0001)
Education: Diploma IV/S1 × Post-democratization	0.02***	0.01***	0.01***	0.01***	0.01***	0.01***
	(0.0002)	(0.0001)	(0.0001)	(0.0002)	(0.0001)	(0.0001)
Education: Post-graduate × Post-democratization	0.03***	0.03***	0.03***	0.03***	0.03***	0.03***
	(0.0004)	(0.0004)	(0.0004)	(0.0004)	(0.0004)	(0.0004)

Table 4 *(Cont.)*

	Promotion (1)	Promotion (2)	Promotion (3)	Promotion (4)	Promotion (5)	Promotion (6)
Controls	Yes	Yes	Yes	Yes	Yes	Yes
Sample	Full	Full	Full	Pre-1999	Pre-1999	Pre-1999
Department FE	Yes	Yes	Yes	Yes	Yes	Yes
Province of birth FE	Yes	No	No	Yes	No	No
Individual FE	No	Yes	Yes	No	Yes	Yes
Golongan FE	No	No	Yes	No	No	Yes
Year FE	Yes	Yes	Yes	Yes	Yes	Yes
N	51,674,834	51,674,834	51,674,834	30,130,880	30,130,880	30,130,880
R^2	0.03	0.20	0.20	0.03	0.18	0.18

Adjusted R^2	0.03	0.14	0.14	0.03	0.15	0.15
Residual std. error	0.12	0.11	0.11	0.11	0.10	0.10
	(df = 51,674,125)	(df = 48,153,553)	(df = 48,153,537)	(df = 30,130,174)	(df = 29,137,554)	(df = 29,137,538)

Notes: ***Significant at the 1% level.
     **Significant at the 5% level.
     *Significant at the 10% level.
     Standard errors are clustered at the individual level.

the sample to individuals hired before 1999, I still find that democratization has statistically and substantively important effects on the premium associated with educational attainment. The increase in the probability of promotion ranges between 1 and 3 percentage points across models and levels of education. The magnitude of effects is ordered as expected: higher premiums are associated with higher educational attainment.

This provides strong support for the main hypothesis, indicating that democratic accountability has dramatically shifted promotion patterns within the civil service and amplified the demand for competence, favoring highly educated individuals.

One possible concern may be that educational attainment proxies for family wealth and access to higher education, and that wealth was more rewarded after democratization – for example, rich individuals could bribe their way up the echelon hierarchy. It could also be the case that the signaling value of educational degrees increased after 1999, for instance due to the influence of international aid organizations. For example, international organizations expressed a strong preference for government counterparts with higher educational credentials. If that were the case, one might observe increases in the returns to education, but not due to an increased demand for competence. One reason the observed patterns are unlikely to solely reflect familial wealth or signaling effects is that the returns to mid-level education and unfinished college degrees also increased. This suggests that competence, and not just acquiring diplomas, is driving these findings.

4.4 Robustness Checks

A series of robustness checks confirms this finding. Instead of using the binary promotion event as my outcome variable, I repeat the estimations in Table 4, using the ordinal echelon level as the dependent variable.[50] This change has no impact on the substantive findings of the effect of democratization when estimated via OLS (see Appendix D) or an ordered-probit model.[51] Using an alternative cluster structure for the standard errors, for instance at the department level, I also corroborate my initial set of results (see Appendix F).

There is also a concern that promotion opportunities vary systematically and over time across departments. While the year fixed effects account for global trends in the number of civil service jobs and promotion opportunities, it

---

[50] I also consider a coarser categorical grouping with five outcomes, combining several of the echelon ranks, and the results remain the same.

[51] For the ordered-probit model I rely on an 8 percent random sample due to memory problems in the estimation. Results are available on request.

could be that there is faster growth in civil service jobs in ministries and district governments that prioritize educational attainment. To address this concern, I estimate the models with department- and province-specific linear time trends, interacting each organizational unit dummy or provincial indicator with a linear year counter. Doing so, I replicate my main results (see Appendix E).

4.4.1 Variation by Year

To test whether the effects of education truly changed as a consequence of the democratization in 1999, I use a flexible specification that interacts the variables of interest with the year dummies. This approach, which follows Angrist & Pischke (2009), allows us to trace changes in the effects of education over the full time period. I estimate the same models as before, but for simplicity, I construct a single dummy variable indicating higher educational attainment, based on whether a civil servant has completed a bachelor's or postgraduate degree. Appendix G shows a table of regression coefficients for the interaction terms. Figure 11 displays the varying differential effect by year above the baseline effects. The pattern strongly supports my initial findings. The figure shows that before 1999 the premium for education was slowly eroding, but year-to-year changes were statistically indistinguishable from one another. In 2001, there was a dramatic upward shift in the education premium. This delay is plausible since the transition to democracy likely took one to two years before any change in the top political leadership had real effects on promotion patterns in the civil service.

4.4.2 Decentralization and Local Elections

While Figure 11 shows a structural break around 2001, in line with an effect of democratization, Indonesia also passed deep structural decentralization reforms that year. These reforms instituted electoral accountability at the local level and transferred primary responsibility for public services like education and health care to the district level, which involved reassigning more than two million civil servants from the central government to the district governments. Although the decentralization reforms increased local political accountability and mirror the country's national-level shift to democracy, an effect driven by political decentralization would be slightly different from a mechanism that is solely driven by competitive elections.

To determine whether this transfer of oversight responsibility was the real driver of changes in promotion patterns, I rerun the regressions excluding individuals who were transferred to district governments from the sample. Appendix H reports the results, which indicate that employees who were

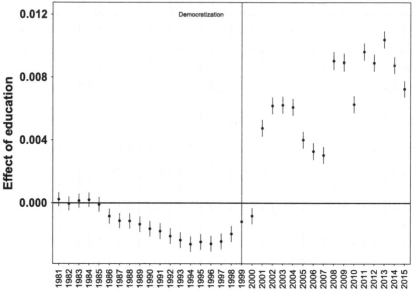

Figure 11 Differential effect of the education premium over the baseline by year

unaffected by the decentralization reforms still experienced an increase in their educational premium. Therefore, I am reasonably confident that an increase in democratic accountability, rather than decentralization, is driving my results.

To further demonstrate that changes to *political accountability* – rather than *decentralization* – are responsible for the findings, I exploit the introduction of direct local elections in 2005. District governments are headed by local mayors who were previously elected indirectly via local legislatures. This process was fraught with political corruption and backroom deals, and produced local leaders who were not particularly accountable to the local population. The 2005 reform created a much more competitive local electoral process (Erb & Sulistiyanto, 2009). I exploit its staggered introduction over a five-year period for identification purposes. The timing of the introduction of direct elections was determined by sitting incumbents' end terms, which in turn depended on their dates of appointment under the Suharto regime. Thus from 2005 onward, district governments successively switched to direct and more competitive local elections, which allows us to generate an exogenously determined treatment indicator. A number of previous studies have exploited this natural experiment (e.g., Pierskalla & Sacks [2018]; Skoufias et al. [2014]). I create a subset from the original panel of civil servants, selecting only district-level employees in the post-2000 period, to test whether the introduction of local elections had a similar impact on the effects of education. Given that district heads are the final arbiters of promotions within district governments and the timing of introducing local direct elections varies across years, I have a powerful design to check the robustness of the initial results.

I estimate the following model:

$$y_{idpgt} = \alpha_i + \gamma_d + \eta_p + \rho_g + \tau_t + \kappa \cdot \mathbf{m_{dt}}$$
$$+ \beta \cdot \text{Edu}_{\mathbf{it}} + \eta \cdot \text{Local Elections}_{dt} + \delta \cdot \text{Local Elections}_{dt} \cdot \text{Edu}_{\mathbf{it}}$$
$$+ \theta \cdot \mathbf{z_{it}} + \epsilon_{idpgt}$$

This model has a similar structure to the initial specification, but includes district government fixed effects γ_d instead of the more general department fixed effects, the same indicator of educational attainment $\text{edu}_{\mathbf{it}}$, the set of individual-level controls $\mathbf{z_{it}}$, and additional, time-varying district-level control variables $\mathbf{m_{dt}}$. I include a dummy variable for incumbent district heads running for re-election, the effective number of parties in the local legislature, the vote share of the Golkar and PDI-P parties in the local legislature, an index of the quality of local services provision,[52] natural resource revenue per capita, total revenue per capita, a Gini index of consumption inequality, logged total district population, the number of people below the poverty line per capita, and logged GDP per capita. The main difference from the prior specification is the inclusion of a time-varying binary indicator of the introduction of local elections, *Elected Leader*, which I also interact with the categorical education measure. I estimate the same set of models as in Table 4, varying the set of fixed effects and excluding post-1999 hires. Table 5 reports the findings.

Similar to the national-level results, the introduction of direct elections shifted the premium of educational attainment. As before, I find that educational attainment increased promotion rates before a district government introduced direct elections. This effect increases and the difference is statistically significant for most educational categories. The finding that the change in effect size is typically smaller than in the national sample is plausible, since democratization already has an overall national effect, and highly educated civil servants have fewer opportunities to advance in district governments compared to national ministries.[53]

---

[52] Based on access to safe water, safe sanitation, enrollment levels, the presence of asphalt roads, and the number of births attended by skilled staff.

[53] Looking at the overall effect of direct elections, the results depend on the sub-type of civil servant. For civil servants with less than 4-years of college, promotion rates slowed, but accelerated for civil servants with four or more years of tertiary education. This is in line with findings by Valsecchi (2016), who makes a related but distinct contribution. He studies the effects of local elections on corruption, as measured by the number of indictments, and aggregate promotion rates of district-level civil servants from 2002–2011. Importantly, his analysis is

Table 5 Promotion analysis: local elections and education

	Promotion	Promotion	Promotion	Promotion	Promotion	Promotion
	(1)	(2)	(3)	(4)	(5)	(6)
Education: Junior High	0.004***			0.004***		
	(0.0005)			(0.001)		
Education: Senior High	0.02***			0.01***		
	(0.0003)			(0.0004)		
Education: Diploma I/II/III	0.01***			0.01***		
	(0.0003)			(0.0004)		
Education: Diploma IV/S1	0.03***			0.02***		
	(0.0003)			(0.0004)		
Education: Post-graduate	0.10***			0.09***		
	(0.001)			(0.001)		

Elected Leader	−0.004***	−0.01***	−0.01***	−0.005***	−0.005***	−0.005***
	(0.0003)	(0.0002)	(0.0002)	(0.0003)	(0.0002)	(0.0002)
Education: Junior High×Elected Leader	−0.0000	0.002***	0.002***	0.002***	0.001***	0.001***
	(0.0005)	(0.0004)	(0.0004)	(0.001)	(0.001)	(0.001)
Education: Senior High×Elected Leader	0.001***	0.004***	0.004***	0.004***	0.005***	0.005***
	(0.0003)	(0.0002)	(0.0002)	(0.0004)	(0.0002)	(0.0002)
Education: Diploma I/II/III×Elected Leader	0.002***	0.001***	0.001***	0.002***	0.001***	0.001***
	(0.0003)	(0.0001)	(0.0001)	(0.0003)	(0.0001)	(0.0001)
Education: Diploma IV/S1×Elected Leader	0.004***	0.01***	0.01***	0.01***	0.005***	0.005***
	(0.0003)	(0.0002)	(0.0002)	(0.0003)	(0.0002)	(0.0002)

Table 5 *(Cont.)*

	Promotion	Promotion	Promotion	Promotion	Promotion	Promotion
	(1)	(2)	(3)	(4)	(5)	(6)
Education: Post-graduate×Elected Leader	0.01***	0.03***	0.03***	0.02***	0.02***	0.02***
	(0.001)	(0.001)	(0.001)	(0.002)	(0.002)	(0.002)
	Promotion	Promotion	Promotion	Promotion	Promotion	Promotion
	(1)	(2)	(3)	(4)	(5)	(6)
Sample	Full	Full	Full	Pre-1999	Pre-1999	Pre-1999
Individual controls	Yes	Yes	Yes	Yes	Yes	Yes
District controls	Yes	Yes	Yes	Yes	Yes	Yes
Department FE	Yes	Yes	Yes	Yes	Yes	Yes
Province of birth FE	Yes	No	No	Yes	No	No
Individual FE	No	Yes	Yes	No	Yes	Yes
Golongan FE	No	No	Yes	No	No	Yes
Year FE	Yes	Yes	Yes	Yes	Yes	Yes

N	10,485,948	10,485,948	10,485,948	5,971,194	5,971,194	5,971,194
R^2	0.03	0.26	0.26	0.04	0.25	0.25
Adjusted R^2	0.03	0.12	0.12	0.04	0.15	0.15
Residual	0.13	0.12	0.12	0.12	0.11	0.11
std. error	(df = 10,485,464)	(df = 8,799,033)	(df = 8,799,017)	(df = 5,970,710)	(df = 5,267,349)	(df = 5,267,333)

Notes: ***Significant at the 1% level.

        **Significant at the 5% level.

        *Significant at the 10% level.

        Standard errors are clustered at the individual level.

4.5 Loyalty and Control

If democratization has a *selection-for-competence* effect on promotions, by implication, I should also observe a relative erosion of the value of loyalty. Ideally, I would like to estimate the returns to loyalty before and after democratization, as with educational attainment. However, it is difficult to measure loyalty to the authoritarian leadership or personal loyalty to the new democratic ruling elite. Since I do not have a direct measure of loyalty, I explore the returns to an indirect proxy for loyalty to the authoritarian regime: being born on Java. For long periods of time, including during the Suharto regime, individuals from the main island of Java have dominated high-level Indonesian politics. I expect that any returns to being originally from Java, rather than the Outer Islands, should have eroded post-1999, as democratization diffused the country's power networks. Appendix I shows that the promotion premium for civil servants born on Java did, in fact, erode post-1999.

The second, more context-specific implication of my argument is that we should also observe an increased demand to control more competent but less loyal civil servants via, for example, the timing of promotions during election years. To test this prediction, I estimate another set of models that capture the change in preelection, election, and postelection year promotion rates before and after 1999. I create a simple binary indicator for national election years – authoritarian elections in 1982, 1987, 1992, 1997 and democratic elections in 1999, 2004, 2009, and 2014. I then construct the necessary lag and lead indicator and interact all three election year dummies with the post-1999 dummy (excluding year effects), using an otherwise unchanged model specification.

Table 6 reports the coefficient estimate for the main models, focusing on (1) differences across preelection, election, and postelection years and (2) changes post-1999.

First, for the constituent term for election years (i.e., the effect of election years under authoritarian rule), the signs vary by model specification. For the more lenient model, which does not include individual-level fixed effects, preelection, election, and postelection years feature more promotions; they feature fewer promotions when individual-level fixed effects are included. The substantive effect is small in both models, and there are no strong differences within the years around the election. This suggests that authoritarian elections were not characterized by massive waves of promotion events, likely because

---

focused on the direct effect of term limits rather than the effects of individual attributes on promotions before and after democratization. His analysis is also based on aggregate district-level data.

Table 6 Promotion analysis: National election year

	Promotion (1)	Promotion (2)	Promotion (3)	Promotion (4)	Promotion (5)	Promotion (6)
Pre-election year	0.002*** (0.0000)	−0.002*** (0.0000)	−0.002*** (0.0000)	0.002*** (0.0000)	−0.001*** (0.0000)	−0.001*** (0.0000)
Election year	0.001*** (0.0000)	−0.001*** (0.0000)	−0.001*** (0.0000)	0.001*** (0.0000)	−0.001*** (0.0000)	−0.001*** (0.0000)
Post-election year	0.001*** (0.0000)	−0.001*** (0.0000)	−0.001*** (0.0000)	0.001*** (0.0000)	−0.001*** (0.0000)	−0.001*** (0.0000)
Post-1999	0.02*** (0.0001)	−0.0003*** (0.0001)	−0.0003*** (0.0001)	0.02*** (0.0001)	0.003*** (0.0001)	0.003*** (0.0001)
Pre-election year*Post-1999	0.001*** (0.0001)	0.003*** (0.0001)	0.003*** (0.0001)	0.001*** (0.0001)	0.003*** (0.0001)	0.003*** (0.0001)

Table 6 *(Cont.)*

	Promotion (1)	Promotion (2)	Promotion (3)	Promotion (4)	Promotion (5)	Promotion (6)
Election year*Post-1999	−0.001***	0.001***	0.001***	−0.002***	0.0004***	0.0004***
	(0.0001)	(0.0001)	(0.0001)	(0.0001)	(0.0001)	(0.0001)
Post-election year*Post-1999	−0.002***	−0.001***	−0.001***	−0.003***	−0.002***	−0.002***
	(0.0001)	(0.0001)	(0.0001)	(0.0001)	(0.0001)	(0.0001)
Sample	Full	Full	Full	Pre-1999	Pre-1999	Pre-1999
Controls	Yes	Yes	Yes	Yes	Yes	Yes
Department FE	Yes	Yes	Yes	Yes	Yes	Yes
Province of birth FE	Yes	No	No	Yes	No	No
Individual FE	No	Yes	Yes	No	Yes	Yes
Golongan FE	No	No	Yes	No	No	Yes

N	51,674,834	51,674,834	51,674,834	30,130,880	30,130,880	30,130,880
R^2	0.02	0.20	0.20	0.03	0.18	0.18
Adjusted R^2	0.02	0.14	0.14	0.03	0.15	0.15
Residual	0.12	0.11	0.11	0.11	0.10	0.10
std. error	(df = 51,674,158)	(df = 48,153,585)	(df = 48,153,569)	(df = 30,130,207)	(df = 29,137,586)	(df = 29,137,570)

Notes: ***Significant at the 1% level.

**Significant at the 5% level.

*Significant at the 10% level.

Standard errors are clustered at the individual level.

civil servants were initially selected based on their loyalty to the regime – thus there was no need to strategically time promotions around election years.

I now turn to the interaction terms to assess changes post-1999, focusing on the models with individual-level fixed effects. I observe statistically significant changes for all three election year dummies. Importantly, these changes are in different directions. Combining interaction terms with the constituent effects, a small positive effect on promotion emerges in the preelection year, a precise zero effect in the election year, and a negative effect for the postelection year.[54] This divergence in effects points toward politically expedient timing around election years: in national election years, promotions increase in the run-up to elections and then decrease. These patterns are consistent with theoretical expectations. Elections during Suharto's rule were not merely staged events, but featured contestation by opposition parties, however circumscribed (Aspinall, 2005). Democratization in 1999 represented a qualitative and substantial shift toward more competition. As Table 6 indicates, electoral cycles during authoritarian periods were not wholly absent but comparatively less pronounced relative to post-1999.

As in the analysis of the education premium, I can also exploit the staggered introduction of local elections to identify local electoral cycles. While this is not a direct test of the secondary observable implication – after all, there were no direct elections under authoritarian rule – a pattern linking promotions to the timing of local elections after the introduction of direct elections would be consistent with local politicians' emerging need to exert control over the civil service.

I estimate district-level models, focusing on the effect of local preelection, election, and postelection years. The results, displayed in Table 7, suggest a pattern of strategically timed promotions for district-level civil servants. In the run-up to an election year, promotion rates drop below baseline and increase after the election. Again, this indicates that promotions are timed strategically around election years, but the district level reflects a different pattern of timing than national-level elections. This is likely because in many local elections, incumbent mayors feel comfortable delaying promotions to induce loyalty because they expect to retain control over the bureaucracy. At the national level, there is more uncertainty with respect to retaining control over specific parts of the bureaucracy due to postelection bargaining and the politics of coalition formation (Slater & Simmons, 2013); thus it is more expedient to offer promotions before a possible loss of power.

---

[54] The results are similar for models that use echelon rank rather than the binary promotion event as the dependent variable (see Appendix J).

Table 7 Promotion analysis: District election cycle

	Promotion	Promotion	Promotion	Promotion	Promotion	Promotion
	(1)	(2)	(3)	(4)	(5)	(6)
Preelection year	−0.001***	−0.001***	−0.001***	−0.001***	−0.001***	−0.001***
	(0.0001)	(0.0001)	(0.0001)	(0.0001)	(0.0002)	(0.0002)
Election year	−0.001***	−0.001***	−0.001***	−0.001***	−0.001***	−0.001***
	(0.0002)	(0.0002)	(0.0002)	(0.0002)	(0.0002)	(0.0002)
Postelection year	0.0004***	0.0003***	0.0003***	0.0004***	0.0004***	0.0004***
	(0.0001)	(0.0001)	(0.0001)	(0.0001)	(0.0002)	(0.0002)
Sample	Full	Full	Full	Pre-1999	Pre-1999	Pre-1999
Controls	Yes	Yes	Yes	Yes	Yes	Yes
Department FE	Yes	Yes	Yes	Yes	Yes	Yes

Table 7 *(Cont.)*

	Promotion	Promotion	Promotion	Promotion	Promotion	Promotion
	(1)	(2)	(3)	(4)	(5)	(6)
Province of birth FE	Yes	No	No	Yes	No	No
Individual FE	No	Yes	Yes	No	Yes	Yes
Golongan FE	No	No	Yes	No	No	Yes
Year FE	Yes	Yes	Yes	Yes	Yes	Yes
N	10,336,662	10,336,662	10,336,662	5,881,420	5,881,420	5,881,420
R^2	0.03	0.26	0.26	0.04	0.25	0.25
Adjusted R^2	0.03	0.12	0.12	0.04	0.15	0.15
Residual	0.13	0.12	0.12	0.12	0.11	0.11
std. error	(df = 10,336,182)	(df = 8,654,458)	(df = 8,654,442)	(df = 5,880,940)	(df = 5,179,044)	(df = 5,179,028)

Notes: ***Significant at the 1% level.
  **Significant at the 5% level.
  *Significant at the 10% level.
  Standard errors are clustered at the individual level.

Further exploiting the local electoral setting, I explore whether the demand for educated civil servants after the introduction of direct elections and the election cycle timing effects are stronger in localities with politics dominated by clientelism.

While I claim that democratization leads to a general preference for competence, I expect the demand for control to be particularly pronounced in electoral environments characterized by clientelism. A growing literature on Indonesian politics has detailed the mechanics of clientelism and vote buying since 1999 (Aspinall, 2014; Aspinall & Sukmajati, 2016; Berenschot, 2018b; Berenschot & Mulder, 2019; Muhtadi, 2019). Aspinall & Berenschot (2019) and Berenschot & Mulder (2019) use qualitative and quantitative evidence to show that the prevalence of clientelistic practices varies across districts.

They find that state dominance over the local economy is a reliable predictor of clientelism. Since clientelism in Indonesia is often facilitated by the bureaucracy, large local governments provide ample resources to organize machines that can deliver votes in competitive local races.[55]

I follow their approach and extend the district-level models with a variable that captures local state dominance – measured as the district budget as a percentage of local GDP. I estimate two sets of models. First, I repeat the model from Section 4.4.2 and include a triple interaction between the introduction of direct elections, educational attainment, and local state dominance. Second, I estimate a district-level model with an interaction between the election year dummies and local government dominance (results reported in Appendix K).

First, I find that the education premium increases even more after the introduction of direct elections in districts with a large government budget. Second, the clustering of promotions in postelection years is especially pronounced in areas with larger governments. Both patterns are in line with a mechanism that associates electoral accountability with (a) a demand for competence and (b) an increased need for control; this is consistent with a local political economy characterized by clientelistic rather than programmatic politics.

Finally, I also consider which civil servants were particularly affected by election cycle effects, by interacting the educational attainment indicator with the election year dummies (see Appendix L). Consistent with my argument

---

[55] On a related note, Berenschot (2018a) argues that electoral competition in Indonesia incentivizes rulers to hire incompetent but loyal civil servants to facilitate clientelism. He uses evidence of widespread corruption in the country's civil service and ethnographic fieldwork to support this claim. My argument is aligned with this perspective in that competitive clientelism makes it more important for politicians to exercise control and discretion over the civil service, which hinders the introduction of depoliticizing reforms. I deviate from Berenschot (2018a) on the dimension of competence. Competence, paired with discretionary control, can be entirely consistent with widespread corruption and mass-level clientelism.

about a trade-off between competence and loyalty, I find that highly educated civil servants are more likely to be promoted in postelection years.

These findings suggest that local civil servants' promotions are at least somewhat politicized. This is in line with the general perception that Indonesia's local civil service reforms have lagged, and that centrally decreed regulations have been implemented unevenly. Direct elections at the local level have created a highly contested political environment, in which candidates have to rely on a variety of resources to win. District-level bureaucracies serve as powerful reservoirs of political, financial, and logistical resources for machine politics in local elections (Berenschot, 2018a; Blunt, Turner, & Lindroth, 2012a, 2012b). Due to the political importance of vote buying and related clientelistic strategies, district heads have a strong incentive to establish control over state resources to leverage in election campaigns. This includes the allegiance and support of civil servants, which provides incentives for district heads to slow or block the application of merit principles in the management of the civil service (Berenschot, 2018a; Sumampouw, 2016). While the central government has tried to curb the politicization of the civil service, civil servants have become an important part of the electoral machinery in many parts of Indonesia (Berenschot, 2018a; Sumampouw, 2016). For example, Regulation No. 53/2010 explicitly prohibits supporting the campaign activities of regional heads and mayors. Likewise, the 2016 Law on Regional Elections No. 10, reinforced by General Election Commission Regulation 2017/3, prohibits incumbent district heads from transferring civil servants six months before or after an election; it has done little to prevent district mayors from threatening to transfer civil servants during electoral periods (Suwitri, Supriyono, & Kuswandaru, 2019).

In related work, co-authored with Audrey Sacks (Pierskalla & Sacks, 2020), we find additional evidence for the increased politicization of the state by studying the education sector. Using comprehensive data on the hiring of contract teachers and the certification of full civil service teachers (which comes with substantial salary rewards), we also find evidence for political distortions in the management of the education sector, tied to the electoral calendar.

The increased politicization of the Indonesian government apparatus is also reflected in the emergence of budgetary expenditure cycles for district governments. Several studies have found evidence of spending patterns that follow the local electoral calendar. For instance, Sjahrir, Kis-Katos, & Schulze (2013) find that discretionary administrative expenditures – which district heads can use flexibly to curry favors – increase in election years. Similarly, Skoufias and colleagues (2014) present evidence that sectoral or functional expenditures increase in election years. Pierskalla & Sacks (2018) document a more subtle phenomenon: election years are associated with temporary drops in capital investment, likely because elections divert administrative attention away from complex infrastructure projects. These findings point to a consistent overall pattern: intense local electoral competition has warped the management and operation of local bureaucracies to serve narrow electoral concerns, thus politicizing the bureaucracy.

5 Democratization and Performance

The previous section provided evidence of the increased demand for competent civil servants in high-level positions in post-1999 Indonesia. I have also provided evidence of the parallel increased politicization of everyday management practices in the civil service. Here I explore whether democratization has also affected government performance. As argued in Section 2, an increased preference for skill and competence does not necessarily translate to more effective or efficient public goods provision. In some contexts, *selection for competence* facilitates mass-level clientelism and patronage; in others, it results in improvements of public goods – either of which could improve the living conditions of at least some citizens. Politicians may even pursue both simultaneously, using competent civil servants to improve service delivery in some areas, while amplifying patronage in other parts of the government.

It is difficult to identify the downstream consequences for the quality of public services provision. Ideally, direct measures of civil servant effort and productivity could shed light on the relationship between increased competence in leadership positions and performance. Yet few countries have such comprehensive data available. It is also challenging to directly measure individual civil servant effort and performance in many subject areas. Most research that has attempted to do so has focused on the provision of frontline services such as health care (e.g., Callen et al. [2015] or Weaver [2021]), teaching and student test scores (e.g., de Ree et al. [2018]), or tax collection (Hasnain, Manning, & Pierskalla, 2014), excluding core areas of the broader civil service (Hasnain, Manning, & Pierskalla, 2014). Assessments based on external, scientific surveys are costly (e.g., see Bertrand et al. [n.d.]). In addition, since teams produce many civil service outputs, and the effects of managers' increased competence ought to materialize at the team or unit level, information on team compositions is needed. While my prior analyses draw on micro-level administrative data on civil servants' educational qualifications, the data do not contain any direct measures of civil servant performance (or perceptions thereof); nor do they allow for a detailed reconstruction of teams and units within larger civil service organizations.

In lieu, this section draws on aggregate measures of government performance. This is not ideal for two reasons. First, a long and complex causal chain links changes in the promotions of educated civil servants as a consequence of democratization to the subsequent delivery of public goods. This makes it challenging to attribute any changes in outcomes and government performance to the role of *selection for competence*. Second, government performance measures are often only available at the national or subnational level, which limits our ability to attribute changes in the advancement of individual competent bureaucrats to outcomes.

Nonetheless, aggregate outcomes helpfully reflect conditions that affect people's well-being. Ultimately, I am trying to determine how democratization reshapes the relationships between political elites, civil servants, and citizens – and what the consequences are for the performance of the public sector. Therefore, it is important and instructive to assess the overall aggregate evidence on government performance, even if we cannot perfectly observe the causal chain from democratization, to changes in internal management practices, to the eventual downstream performance of governments writ large.

In the following, I broadly assess how the performance of the public sector has changed in Indonesia since 1999. First, I provide descriptive evidence on national-level trends in government performance, drawing on expert and citizens' perceptions-based assessments of government quality, data on corruption indictments from official government sources, and aggregate indicators of public goods provision. Second, I use the synthetic control method approach to determine to what extent any national-level changes in quality of government can be attributed to democratization. Third, I use the staggered introduction of direct elections at the subnational level to test if more competitive elections have shifted government expenditures and service delivery outcomes. Finally, I use subnational data on local government's civil servants to determine if competence played a role in changing government outputs.

5.1 National-Level Trends in Government Quality and Performance

I start by broadly assessing the organizational quality of Indonesia's civil service at the national level. Section 3 detailed a number of specific post-democratization organizational and regulatory changes within the civil service. Here I evaluate the quality of Indonesia's civil service in terms of governance and meritocracy. Past studies have relied on a number of aggregate proxy measures to capture a country's overall quality of government; many have severe measurement problems, are difficult to compare over time, or do not provide any data points for Indonesia prior to 1999.[56] The V-Dem project provides a suitable measurement (Coppedge et al., 2019). This project relies on a large set of country experts to collect scores on several regime characteristics across countries and historical time periods. Expert judgments are combined via a Bayesian measurement model to produce a series of useful and comparable indicator measures (Pemstein, Tzelgov, & Wang, 2015). To start, I focus on experts' perceptions of overall political corruption, executive corruption, executive bribery, and executive embezzlement (see Figure 12). These indicators assess the degree of top-level political and executive corruption to give a sense of how political elites have adapted their rent seeking in Indonesia's changing political environment.

The two top panels of Figure 12 show that overall perceptions of corruption declined around 1999. Interestingly, while the top-line indicators of corruption indicate a decline, more specific measures of executive bribery and embezzlement (bottom two panels) show an increase. This contrast is repeated for corruption in the public sector: while expert assessments of overall public sector corruption declined around 1999, the number of corrupt exchanges and public sector theft increased – panels (b) and (c) in Figure 13. Moving from perceptions of public sector corruption to more direct assessments of meritocracy, V-Dem's indicator of meritocracy in the civil service – a zero to four ordinal measure that measures to what extent public sector appointments are based on skill and merit – suggests a noticeable improvement in Indonesia's public sector (panel (d) in Figure 13). This is consistent with the moderate effort to pass laws and implement regulations that anchor meritocratic norms in the civil service and my findings in Section 4.

The apparent contradiction of patterns revealed by aggregate corruption indicators is likely due to a qualitative shift in the type of corruption in Indonesia after 1999. Patronage and corruption in the civil service were previously centralized under the control of Suharto and his inner circle (McLeod, 2000, 2008). Private sector fortunes rose and fell depending on individuals' personal connections to the Suharto family and his perceived health (and ability to hold onto power) (Fisman, 2001). Democratization brought change, dismantling the infamous "franchise system" of corruption and patronage, but ushered in a new period of decentralized corruption

---

[56] For example, the World Bank's Ease of Doing Business Index (www.doingbusiness.org/) offers an overall assessment of the local regulatory environment, but has been mired in serious controversies and measurement problems (Sandefur & Wadhwa, 2018). The construction of Transparency International's Corruption Perception Index makes over-time comparisons difficult.

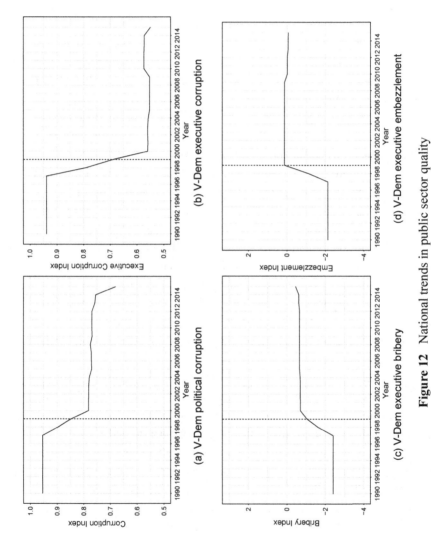

Figure 12 National trends in public sector quality

Note: Each panel displays an index from the V-Dem project.

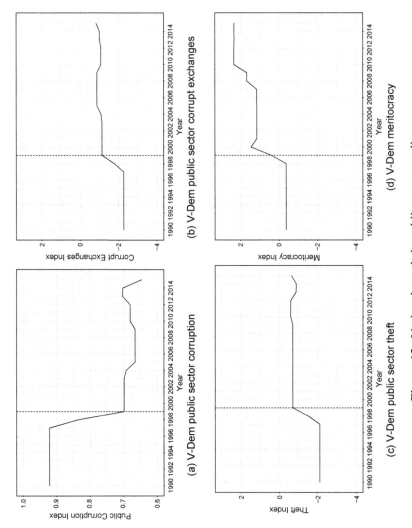

Figure 13 National trends in public sector quality

Table 8 KPK investigations 2002–2016

Type	Cases	Share
Elected official	50	0.14
Legislator	60	0.17
Local civil servant	60	0.17
National civil servant	30	0.08
State-owned enterprise official	30	0.08
Private sector	98	0.27
Minister	6	0.02
Judicial	19	0.05

(Aspinall & Sukmajati, 2016; Blunt, Turner, & Lindroth, 2012a, 2012b; Hadiz, 2010; McLeod, 2008; Mietzner, 2018b; Robison & Hadiz, 2004).

Concerted efforts to combat corruption have had only mixed success. With strong backing from civil society, the Indonesian Anti-Corruption Commission (*Komisi Pemberantasan Korupsi*, KPK) was created to facilitate the investigation and prosecution of government corruption after the transition. Lauded for its efforts, the KPK has certainly worked hard to identify and prosecute corruption in Indonesia. Between its creation in 2002 and 2016, based on its published reports, the KPK has investigated more than 350 individuals for corruption. These cases are not necessarily representative of corruption more generally, since it uses prosecutorial and political judgment in which leads to follow and cases to pursue. As such, KPK corruption cases are not perfect measures of corruption in Indonesia. Nonetheless, the body of cases reveals some noteworthy patterns. Of those investigated, 72 percent were public officials and 28 percent private individuals – often involving the bribery of public officials to obtain public procurement contracts or government licenses. Table 8 displays a more detailed breakdown of cases; 25 percent of cases pertain to civil servants at the local and national levels, and another 31 percent to legislators or elected officials like mayors or governors. This demonstrates that corruption cases pursued by the KPK often focus on politicians and their civil servant collaborators, which together represent a fairly broad class of actors – not simply a single autocrat and their family. This is consistent with the removal of Suharto's system of centralized corruption and its replacement by a more decentralized system of widespread corruption, implicating a broad class of politicians and government actors.

This shift toward decentralized corruption networks is also evidenced by the increased political headwinds for the KPK. Despite a number of high-profile indictments and early successes, Indonesia's political elite, especially representatives in the national parliament, has soured on the commission's independence and zeal. Recent actions by the incumbent Widodo government and the national parliament have undermined its effectiveness (Lindsey, 2019). In contrast to the KPK's national-level anti-corruption efforts, local investigations and prosecutions are highly politicized – often weaponized in inter-elite rivalries rather than driven by a desire for good governance (Tomsa, 2015).

In contrast to expert assessments, there is no survey data that could be used to reliably compare citizens' perceptions of the quality of government and access to public services before and after 1999, Asia Barometer provides reliable survey data for the post-democratization period (in 2006, 2011, and 2016). Each survey wave included four questions about access to basic government services, measured from 1 = (very difficult) to 4 = (very easy). It asked "Based on your experience, how easy or difficult is it to obtain the following services? Or have you never tried to get these services from government?" with specific answer options – "An identity document (such as a birth certificate or passport)," "A place in a public primary school for a child," "Medical treatment at a nearby clinic," and "Help from the police when you need it." Figure 14 shows the average responses. For all four services, respondents scored access between "difficult" and "easy"; police and schools scored lower than access to medical clinics and ID cards. The average responses remained remarkably stable across survey waves. While the data say nothing about citizens' perceptions of government services before 1999, there does not seem to be a noticeable increase in ease of access from 2006 to 2016.

The survey also includes questions on trust in government institutions. Respondents were asked to rate their level of trust in a series of government institutions, ranging from 1 (none at all) to 4 (a great deal of trust).[57] Figure 15 displays the average levels of trust in the civil service and a number of other public institutions (the courts, local government, the military, parliament, the police). In 2006, the civil service received an average score of 3.00 (i.e., "quite a lot of trust"). Since then, average perceptions have fallen to 2.79 in 2011 and 2.81 in 2016. This suggests that citizens' lived experience of interactions with the Indonesian bureaucracy after democratization is not solely a story of improved governance. A similar erosion in public trust applies to the courts, parliament, and the police. Slight improvements in trust are recorded for local governments (which gained a lot of responsibility for service delivery

---

[57] The original scale in the survey is reversed: I recoded the responses so that higher numbers indicate higher levels of trust.

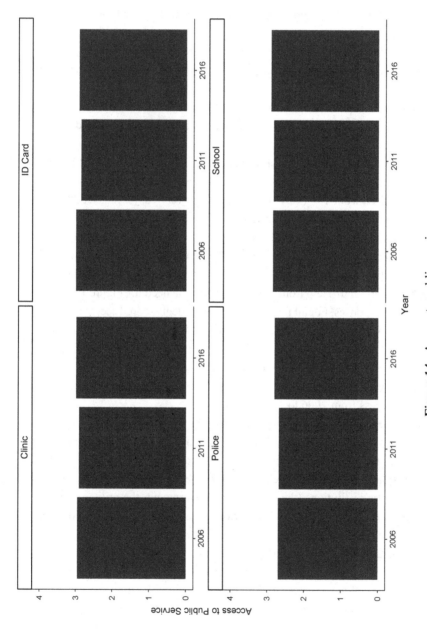

Figure 14 Access to public services

Note: Self-reported level of access to public health clinics, government ID cards, the police, and schools from Asia Barometer.

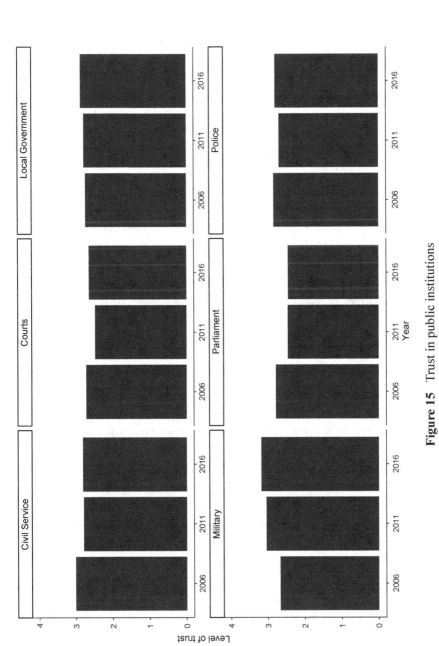

Figure 15 Trust in public institutions

Note: Displays trust in the civil service, courts, local government, the military, parliament, and the police from Asia Barometer.

that directly impacts citizens' lives) and the military. It is notable that the civil service was the most trusted public institution in 2006 but has since lost this distinction.

Overall, this paints a somewhat positive, albeit mixed, picture of expert and citizens' assessments of the quality of governance in Indonesia. What about the quality of service delivery? Figure 16 displays national trends for four important proxies for government performance between 1996 and 2015: secondary school enrollment rates (World Development Indicators), life expectancy at birth (World Development Indicators), the rate of measles immunization (World Development Indicators), and infant mortality (World Health Organization).[58]

All four metrics display an overall improvement, especially secondary school enrollment rates and infant mortality. However, it is difficult to determine whether this secular trend toward better public goods provision and quality of life is due to democratization. Unlike measures of public sector quality, none of the indicators in Figure 16 displays a visible trend break around 1999. The observed gains might simply be due to unrelated trends – for example, driven by economic growth, foreign aid flows, or technological advancement – and wholly separate from democratization.

5.2 Synthetic Control and National-Level Performance

One approach to answering this counterfactual question relies on the synthetic control method (Abadie, 2021; Abadie, Diamond, & Hainmueller, 2010). We would like to know how Indonesia would have performed on the four indicators if democratization had not occurred in 1999. The synthetic control approach uses other empirical cases to construct a "synthetic" version of Indonesia to simulate this counterfactual. By constructing a weighted average of other countries that replicates Indonesia's actual trends before 1999, this synthetic version of Indonesia represents an interesting comparison to the observed developments post-1999. Pepinsky & Wihardja (2011) use this approach to quantify the effects of Indonesia's decentralization reforms on economic growth. I follow their example and construct a synthetic control of Indonesia, relying on their sample and data on 69 developing countries. I use measures of trade openness, a binary indicator for the occurrence of a financial crisis, urbanization rates, the Herfindahl index of ethnic fractionalization, log GDP per capita, and

---

[58] Several prior studies have used these to proxy for the quality of government (Dahlum & Knutsen, 2017; Gerring, Thacker, & Alfaro, 2012; Hanson, 2015; Harding, 2019; Kudamatsu, 2012; Ross, 2006; Shandra et al., 2003).

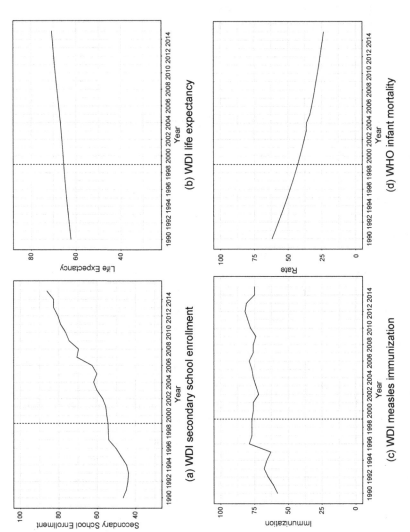

Figure 16 National trends in public service delivery

annual inflation rates as covariates to construct a synthetic version of Indonesia that most closely approximates its pre-1999 characteristics. Figure 17 graphs the actual versus counterfactual service delivery trends (i.e., if democratization had not happened in 1999). Only secondary school enrollment rates outperform the synthetic control version of Indonesia after 2006 (panel (a)). For life expectancy and infant mortality, there is no discernible difference between the real and synthetic versions. This suggests that any improvements in public health during the 2000s and 2010s were driven by factors unrelated to the macro-level political changes after 1999. Panel (c) in Figure 17 shows the real Indonesia *underperforming* relative to the counterfactual on the rate of measles immunization. Using the synthetic control method generates no clear evidence of strong gains (or losses) in the quality of public service delivery or quality of life as a consequence of democratization.

5.3 Subnational Evidence on Government Performance

The evidence presented thus far has been mixed. While there have been real improvements in overall public service delivery, quality of life, and experts' perceptions of certain governance metrics, there is no strong evidence that positive gains are due to democratization. Moreover, citizens do not seem to have experienced a shift to improved governance and clean government. It is therefore difficult to ascertain any macro-level effects of democratization on the quality of government in Indonesia. Luckily, we can draw on the varied subnational experiences of the country's local governments to shed additional light on this question. As outlined in prior sections, Indonesia implemented wide-ranging decentralization reforms that delegated responsibility for essential government services to the district government level. In addition, the staggered introduction of competitive, direct elections in 2005 substantially changed the local political environment. The varied experiences of district governments in Indonesia after 2001 thus present a useful additional opportunity to understand how democratization affects the quality of government.

I begin by evaluating the effects of direct elections on an important input dimension of public services provision: expenditures. Did the introduction of local direct elections change the expenditure patterns of local governments? I use models similar to the analyses in Section 4 – estimating OLS models with district and year fixed effects, including a battery of time-varying control variables.[59] Appendix M reports tables for the estimated effect of direct elections on total expenditures, personnel expenditures, goods and services, and capital

---

[59] I include log GDP per capita, the Gini consumption index, log population, total revenue per capita, natural resource revenue per capita, the effective number of parties in the local

Table 11 Professionalism

	Total score	Percent reporting
	(1)	(2)
CS education	3.90***	0.03*
	(1.50)	(0.02)
Control variables	Yes	Yes
N	195	195
R^2	0.12	0.39
Adjusted R^2	0.08	0.36
Residual std. error	4.97 (df = 185)	0.03 (df = 185)

Notes: ***Significant at the 1% level.
**Significant at the 5% level.
*Significant at the 10% level.

accountability, increases services provision, with the exception of the index of service delivery and secondary school enrollment rates. Note that this analysis does not distinguish between clientelistic and programmatic competition. A model that includes a triple interaction between the direct elections binary variable, civil servants' educational attainment, and government size produces mixed results. For some outcomes it suggests that direct elections, paired with competent civil servants, in a programmatic environment improves outcomes (e.g., for immunization rates and secondary school enrollment), but for other dependent variables no clear patterns emerge.

The analysis of subnational patterns complements the assessment of national trends; the former finds that the effects of democratization on actual government performance are mixed and context dependent. While Section 4 provides strong evidence of a general *selection-for-competence* effect and the increased desire to control civil servants, these forces do not linearly map onto improved or worsened public sector outputs.

Do these broad, quantitative patterns comport with more qualitative assessments? A brief look at Indonesia's education sector is instructive. Indonesia's education sector has gone through wide-reaching changes in the last two decades. Being a key government service, employing over 50 percent of all civil servants, it represents a good testing ground to consider the effects of democratization on the performance of the state. During the Suharto regime, the provision of education was the direct responsibility of the central government.

Table 12 Democracy and service delivery

	Services provision	Poverty	Births	Morbidity	Immu	Enroll
	(1)	(2)	(3)	(4)	(5)	(6)
CS education	0.54	−0.01	−0.49	10.33**	6.07	−4.73
	(0.66)	(0.02)	(5.00)	(4.11)	(5.79)	(6.02)
Direct elections	−3.45***	−0.03	−8.41	−1.53	−2.45	−18.75*
	(1.29)	(0.05)	(11.88)	(9.78)	(7.74)	(9.76)
CS education*	0.82***	0.01	2.01	−0.04	0.75	4.35**
Direct elections	(0.29)	(0.01)	(2.68)	(2.22)	(1.74)	(2.17)
Control variables	Yes	Yes	Yes	Yes	Yes	Yes
District FE	Yes	Yes	Yes	Yes	Yes	Yes
Year FE	Yes	Yes	Yes	Yes	Yes	Yes
N	1,427	1,599	1,590	1,591	1,304	702
R^2	0.95	0.94	0.92	0.72	0.77	0.89
Adjusted R^2	0.94	0.93	0.90	0.66	0.72	0.84
Residual std. error	0.76 (df = 1,166)	0.02 (df = 1,322)	6.34 (df = 1,318)	4.87 (df = 1,319)	4.42 (df = 1,061)	2.38 (df = 477)

Table 12 *(Cont.)*

	Electricity	Roads	Water	Sanitation	Violence
	(1)	(2)	(3)	(4)	(5)
CS education	15.91***	−6.33	−0.62	−0.80	19.18
	(4.68)	(11.98)	(4.52)	(8.25)	(27.30)
Direct elections	31.19**	−30.88	−8.88	−11.49	39.88
	(13.21)	(27.43)	(11.46)	(9.30)	(109.31)
CS education*Direct elections	−6.94**	7.01	2.09	2.76	−10.03
	(2.97)	(6.29)	(2.60)	(2.11)	(26.51)
Control variables	Yes	Yes	Yes	Yes	Yes
District FE	Yes	Yes	Yes	Yes	Yes
Year FE	Yes	Yes	Yes	Yes	Yes
N	1,440	602	1,591	1,592	332
R^2	0.95	0.95	0.87	0.91	0.88
Adjusted R^2	0.93	0.91	0.84	0.90	0.84
Residual std. error	4.55 (df = 1,169)	7.40 (df = 351)	6.60 (df = 1,319)	4.90 (df = 1,320)	27.03 (df = 235)

Notes: ***Significant at the 1% level.
**Significant at the 5% level.
*Significant at the 10% level.

Democratization in 1999, the subsequent decentralization reforms, and the 2005 Teacher Law upended this status quo. These reforms made district governments responsible for primary and secondary education, professionalized hiring standards for teachers, introduced salary increases, and led to a substantial expansion of the teaching force, producing comparatively low student–teacher ratios (Cerdan-Infantes et al., 2013).[60] While these reforms in the wake of democratization poured resources into the education system and increasingly focused on the competence of the teaching force, actual learning outcomes have not improved (Chang et al., 2013). In part, this is due to the increased politicization of the education system (Pierskalla & Sacks, 2020). Principals and teachers have increasingly become part of electoral machines and networks that mobilize votes in local elections (ACDP Indonesia, 2015; Rosser & Fahmi, 2016; Rosser & Sulistiyanto, 2013). In a study of teacher hiring in Indonesia (Pierskalla & Sacks, 2020), we show that local elections have led to electoral cycles in the hiring of contract teachers and the certification process for civil servant teachers.[61] Politicians, especially district heads, exert power over teachers by using reassignments and rotations as a tool for punishment (ACDP Indonesia, 2015; Rosser & Fahmi, 2016).

Democratization's effect on the public sector in Indonesia seems to have led to more expenditures across a variety of sectors, modest improvements in human well-being in some areas, decentralized corruption, and the emergence of a competent but strongly politicized public sector that is increasingly linked to local clientelistic machines.

6 Conclusion

Democratization changes the civil service. Does it increase meritocracy and improve the performance of the state? Or does it weaken state capacity? Using competitive elections to select leaders in charge of the state apparatus neither produces a uniform push toward a Weberian state nor does it automatically cannibalize state capacity. Democratization produces nuanced effects on the management of the civil service in terms of who is elevated to positions of power and to what end they are being deployed.

---

[60] In fact, a constitutional amendment requires the Indonesian government to dedicate at least 20 percent of its budget to education.

[61] Teachers can become certified by documenting certain educational requirements or completing a training program, making them eligible for a substantial salary boost. The program was meant to professionalize the workforce by linking high-powered financial incentives with skills acquisition. A randomized-controlled trial evaluation has found no evidence the certification program works as intended (de Ree et al., 2018).

I argue that electoral accountability fundamentally changes how politicians oversee and manage the civil service. While authoritarian leaders typically value personal loyalty over competence, electorally accountable politicians will pursue *selection for competence*; characteristics like educational attainment will become more salient in promotion decisions. This move toward competence increases the civil service's capacity to deliver and implement policy at scale – be it public goods or targeted benefits. The trade-off between personal loyalty and competence also implies that democratization requires politicians to engage in more active monitoring and sanctioning of bureaucrats. While autocrats minimize agency problems by selecting trustworthy but comparatively incompetent agents, electorally accountable politicians have to rely on management tools like promotions and reassignments to align civil servant behavior with their goals. One effective tool is to time promotions to coincide with the electoral calendar to maximize effort and compliance in politically crucial times. Democratization increases the salience of competence in the management of the civil service at the cost of generating electoral cycles in promotions. This argument clarifies that democratization leads to neither purely meritocratic nor purely clientelistic changes in the civil service, but instead features both elements of meritocratic selection and increased politicization and discretionary control in the management of the civil service.

Given this dual nature of the effect of democratization, downstream consequences for the quality of service delivery are context dependent. Democratization that leads to programmatic politics will improve state performance because increasingly competent civil servants are directed by electorally accountable leaders to implement policy changes that reflect their preferred mix of public goods and services. Democratization that leads to competitive elections characterized by clientelism will experience increasingly competent civil servants being directed by electorally accountable leaders to deliver targeted goods as part of machine politics. Whether that increases or decreases measures of citizen welfare relative to authoritarian rule is unclear.

I test my argument using a unique natural experiment in Indonesia. The country's sudden and unplanned transition to democracy in 1999 allows me to compare promotion practices during and after authoritarian rule. I use detailed, micro-level information on all active civil servants in Indonesia as of 2015 to study the effects of education before and after 1999, only relying on within-individual variation. I find clear evidence that the premium for educational attainment has increased substantially post-1999. In practical terms, this means that highly educated civil servants had a better chance of attaining important management positions in Indonesia's civil service after 1999 than before. At the same time, I find that promotions have become more politicized, by being tied to the electoral calendar. These findings reflect how *competence* and *control* both are consequences of democratization.

This movement to increased *selection for competence* and politicization of the bureaucracy has had mixed effects on the quality of governance and service delivery. While Indonesia's record on good governance has improved in some ways, such as through updated regulations and laws and in the perceptions of experts, there is no evidence that the quality of government has improved in the eyes of regular citizens. There are also strong indications that decentralized corruption has intensified, involving numerous local and national state officials, politicians, and judges, while institutions aimed at investigating and prosecuting corruption being increasingly weakened and politicized. In the arena of electoral politics, powerful, patronage-ridden clientelistic machines have emerged, serving as vehicles of influence for wealthy businessmen and dynastic politics (Aspinall & Berenschot, 2019; Robison & Hadiz, 2004).

The impact of democratization on service delivery performance is equally mixed. While a variety of metrics reveal improved living conditions and service delivery outcomes for Indonesian households since 1999, there is only weak evidence tying these impacts to democratization writ large. In other words, while welfare outcomes have improved in Indonesia during democratic rule, the majority of these gains are due to economic growth and other secular changes, and not directly attributable to specific effects of democratization. Looking at the subnational level, my analyses in Section 5 suggest that competitive direct elections have led to more expenditures of district governments (e.g., on health care) and a preference for more educated civil servants. There is also some tentative evidence that where direct elections are paired with a highly educated civil service, better outcomes ensue. This is in line with my theoretical expectations. Democratization has immediate consequences for the human resources dimension of the civil service. Electorally accountable political elites will employ different strategies than their authoritarian counterparts to manage the civil service. How these different management practices translate into downstream service delivery outcomes depends on other contextual factors, such as the prevalence of programmatic or clientelistic linkage strategies. I generally find that areas where the local economy is dominated by the state, an indirect proxy for the prevalence of clientelism, enjoy weaker gains from direct elections paired with a more competent civil service.

These results bear important lessons for the viability of administrative reforms. Public sector reforms have become a key component of good governance programs and enjoy widespread support in the donor community. Indonesia, like many other low and middle income countries, has followed the pressure and advice of Western governments and international donor organizations and implemented a number of de jure reforms of its civil service. Skeptics may perceive such reforms as often being mere theater and a form of doomed-to-fail institutional mimicry (Andrews, Pritchett, & Woolcock, 2017). Changing civil service laws is difficult but nonetheless meaningless if actual practices defy official regulations. My analyses suggest that this level of dire scepticism is not wholly warranted. Competitive elections can produce strong substantive incentives to change every-day management practices in the civil service toward valuing competence. This means that electoral accountability is an important external support pillar for successful public sector reform, generating the right political incentives to match the merit prescriptions of formal civil service reforms with actual practice.

At the same time, competitive elections alone are not enough to produce a competent and politically impartial, autonomous civil service. In fact, the pressures of competitive elections can worsen the politicization of the state bureaucracy, even amplifying sectarian, ethnic or gender biases (Pierskalla et al., 2021), while simultaneously increasing its competence. Electoral pressures push politicians to leverage their control over civil servants' careers to further their political goals, counteracting common normative ideals of an impartial and autonomous state. What are the conditions that mitigate these less desirable implications of electoral accountability? For one, when competitive elections play out in an environment of programmatic politics, democratic accountability may actually translate into better performance in terms of public goods provision and minimize the need to politicize the management of bureaucrats. What does this mean for the viability of public sector reforms? This implies that any reforms of the civil service have to be evaluated in the broader political context and often require accompanying political reforms. For Indonesia, many observers have identified the move toward an open-list voting system and a poor campaign finance law as important contributing factors in the rise of electoral clientelism, weak programmatic party politics, personalism, and vote buying in Indonesian politics (Aspinall & Berenschot, 2019; Mietzner, 2014). These broader political context factors have shaped the exact nature of electoral politics and, by extension, created a distinct pattern of increased competence and control in the civil service. Any attempt to depoliticize the civil service has to start with a look at the electoral environment. Without reforms of the electoral system, any isolated attempt at civil service reform is likely to fall prey to the political incentives elected politicians are subject to. More broadly, popular public sector reform ideas, ranging from modernized entrance exams, training programs, or performance pay have to contend with the reality that elected politicians will use their influence over management practices to further their political goals.

To conclude, it is worth considering the generalizability of my argument and findings. While my claims are specific to Indonesia, its experience is not atypical in the developing world. Its large and important state apparatus and history of autocratic rule make it a useful case to compare the internal operation of a civil service under dictatorship versus democracy in low- to medium-income countries. I broadly expect democratization to produce similar effects in other cases, especially when transitioning from more personalist forms of authoritarian rule that featured cronyism. What about other forms of authoritarian rule? Levitsky & Way (2010) have identified competitive authoritarianism as an increasingly common form of nondemocratic rule. Given that competitive authoritarianism features multiple opposition parties competing in managed, but not fully staged elections, I expect such regimes to experience much smaller effects on the state bureaucracy as a consequence of democratization. While democratization may still increase the preference for competence and desire for control, it will be more difficult to observe a marked difference to pre-democratization practices because competitive authoritarian regimes will have already adopted some preference for competence and control relative to other forms of dictatorial rule.

Finally, while democratization is one mechanism through which the civil service can be nudged toward meritocracy, it is not the only one. As discussed briefly in Section 2, some authoritarian regimes implement *selection for competence* in the absence of competitive elections. This could be the case because such regimes have a more intense need to deliver economic development, because they face a general lack of patronage resources, or because they can depend on a strongly institutionalized ruling party to deliver regime stability instead of having to rely on cronyism. I leave it to future work to discern the effects of democratization in other settings and the ways in which changes to the management of the civil service actually translate to public goods provision, patronage, and the prevalence of corruption.

References

Aaskoven, L., & Nyrup, J. (2021). Performance and Promotions in an Autocracy: Evidence from Nazi Germany. *Comparative Politics, 54*(1), 51–85. https://doi.org/10.5129/001041521X16132218140269.

Abadie, A. (2021). Using Synthetic Controls: Feasibility, Data Requirements, and Methodological Aspects. *Journal of Economic Literature, 59*(2), 391–425. https://doi.org/10.1257/jel.20191450.

Abadie, A., Diamond, A., & Hainmueller, J. (2010). Synthetic Control Methods for Comparative Case Studies: Estimating the Effect of California's Tobacco Control Program. *Journal of the American Statistical Association, 105*(490), 493–505.

ACDP Indonesia. (2015). Teachers Politicized Toward Local Elections. https://janpierskalla.files.wordpress.com/2022/09/appendix__democratization_and_the_state.pdf

Andrews, M., Pritchett, L., & Woolcock, M. J. V. (2017). *Building State Capability: Evidence, Analysis, Action.* Oxford University Press.

Angrist, J. D., & Pischke, J.-S. (2009). *Mostly Harmless Econometrics.* Princeton University Press.

Asian Development Bank. (2021). *A Diagnostic Study of the Civil Service in Indonesia.* https://doi.org/10.22617/TCS210016-2.

Aspinall, E. (2005). *Opposing Suharto: Compromise, Resistance, and Regime Change in Indonesia.* Stanford University Press.

Aspinall, E. (2014). When Brokers Betray: Clientelism, Social Networks, and Electoral Politics in Indonesia. *Critical Asian Studies, 46*(4), 545–570. https://doi.org/10.1080/14672715.2014.960706.

Aspinall, E., & Berenschot, W. (2019). *Democracy for Sale: Elections, Clientelism, and the State in Indonesia.* Cornell University Press.

Aspinall, E., Fossati, D., Muhtadi, B., & Warburton, E. (2019). Elites, Masses, and Democratic Decline in Indonesia. *Democratization, 27*(4), 505–526. https://doi.org/10.1080/13510347.2019.1680971.

Aspinall, E., & Mietzner, M. (2019). Southeast Asia's Troubling Elections: Nondemocratic Pluralism in Indonesia. *Journal of Democracy, 30*(4), 104–118.

Aspinall, E., & Sukmajati, (Eds.). (2016). *Electoral Dynamcis in Indonesia: Money Politics, Patronage and Clientelism at the Grassroots.* National University of Singapore Press.

Bachtiar, H. W. (1972). Bureaucracy and Nation Formation in Indonesia. *Bijdragen tot de Taal-, Land- en Volkenkunde, 128*(4), 430–446.

Bäck, H., & Hadenius, A. (2008). Democracy and State Capacity: Exploring a J-Shaped Relationship. *Governance, 21*(1), 1–24. https://doi.org/10.1111/j.1468-0491.2007.00383.x.

Bai, Y., & Jia, R. (2016). Elite Recruitment and Political Stability: The Impact of the Abolition of China's Civil Service Exam. *Econometrica, 84*(2), 677–733. https://doi.org/10.3982/ECTA13448.

Banuri, S., & Keefer, P. (2016). Pro-social Motivation, Effort and the Call to Public Service. *European Economic Review, 83*, 139–164. https://doi.org/10.1016/j.euroecorev.2015.10.011.

Banuri, S., & Keefer, P. (2015). *Was Weber Right? The Effects of Pay for Ability and Pay for Performance on Pro-social Motivation, Ability and Effort in the Public Sector* (Tech. Rep. No. WPS7261). The World Bank.

Berenschot, W. (2018a). Incumbent Bureaucrats: Why Elections Undermine Civil Service Reform in Indonesia. *Public Administration and Development, 38*(4), 135–143. https://doi.org/10.1002/pad.1838.

Berenschot, W. (2018b). The Political Economy of Clientelism: A Comparative Study of Indonesia's Patronage Democracy. *Comparative Political Studies, 51*(12), 1563–1593. https://doi.org/10.1177/0010414018758756.

Berenschot, W., & Mulder, P. (2019). Explaining Regional Variation in Local Governance: Clientelism and State-Dependency in Indonesia. *World Development, 122*, 233–244. https://doi.org/10.1016/j.worlddev.2019.05.021.

Berliner, D., & Erlich, A. (2015). Competing for Transparency: Political Competition and Institutional Reform in Mexican States. *American Political Science Review, 109*(1), 110–128. https://doi.org/10.1017/S0003055414000616.

Bertrand, M., Burgess, R., Chawla, A., & Xu, G. (2020). The Glittering Prizes: Career Incentives and Bureaucrat Performance. *The Review of Economic Studies, 87*(2), 626–655. https://doi.org/10.1093/restud/rdz029.

Berwick, E., & Christia, F. (2016). State Capacity Redux: Integrating Classical and Experimental Contributions to an Enduring Debate. *Annual Review of Political Science, 21*, 71–91.

Beschel, R., Cameron, B. J., Kunicova, J., & Myers, C. B. (2018). *Improving Public Sector Performance: Through Innovation and Inter-Agency Coordination* (Tech. Rep. No. 131020). The World Bank.

Besley, T. (2006). *Principled Agents? The Political Economy of Good Government.* Oxford University Press.

Besley, T., & Burgess, R. (2002). The Political Economy of Government Responsiveness: Theory and Evidence from India. *Quarterly Journal of Economics, 117*(4), 1415–1451.

Besley, T., & Reynal-Querol, M. (2011). Do Democracies Select More Educated Leaders? *American Political Science Review, 105*(3), 552–566. https://doi.org/10.1017/S0003055411000281.

Best, M. C., Hjort, J., & Szakonyi, D. (2019). *Individuals and Organizations as Sources of State Effectiveness, and Consequences for Policy* (Working Paper No. 23350). National Bureau of Economic Research.

Bhavnani, R. R., & Lee, A. (2017). Local Embeddedness and Bureaucratic Performance: Evidence from India. *The Journal of Politics, 80*(1), 71–87. https://doi.org/10.1086/694101.

Blaydes, L. (2011). *Elections and Distributive Politics in Mubarak's Egypt.* Cambridge University Press.

Blunt, P., Turner, M., & Lindroth, H. (2012a). Patronage, Service Delivery, and Social Justice in Indonesia. *International Journal of Public Administration, 35*(2), 214–220.

Blunt, P., Turner, M., & Lindroth, H. (2012b). Patronage's Progress in Post-Soeharto Indonesia. *Public Administration and Development, 32*, 64–81.

Bockstette, V., Chanda, A., & Putterman, L. (2002). States and Markets: The Advantage of an Early Start. *Journal of Economic Growth, 7*, 347–369.

Brambor, T., Goenaga, A., Lindvall, J., & Teorell, J. (2020). The Lay of the Land: Information Capacity and the Modern State. *Comparative Political Studies, 53*(2), 175–213. https://doi.org/10.1177/0010414019843432.

Brierley, S. (2020). Combining Patronage and Merit in Public Sector Recruitment. *The Journal of Politics, 81*(1), 182–197. https://doi.org/10.1086/708240.

Buehler, M. (2010). Decentralisation and Local Democracy in Indonesia: The Marginalisation of the Public Sphere. In E. Aspinall & M. Mietzner (Eds.), *Problems of Democratisation in Indonesia: Elections, Institutions and Society* (pp. 267–285). ISEAS.

Buehler, M. (2016). *The Politics of Shari'a Law: Islamist Activists and the State in Democratizing Indonesia.* New York: Cambridge University Press.

Callen, M., Gulzar, S., Hasanain, A., Khan, Y., & Rezaee, A. (2015). *Personalities and Public Sector Performance: Evidence from a Health Experiment in Pakistan* (Working Paper No. 21180). National Bureau of Economic Research.

Callen, M., Gulzar, S., Hasanain, S. A., & Khan, M. Y. (2016). *The Political Economy of Public Sector Absence: Experimental Evidence from Pakistan* (Working Paper No. 22340). National Bureau of Economic Research.

Card, D. (1999). The Causal Effect of Education on Earnings. *Handbook of Labor Economics, 3,* 1801–1863. https://doi.org/10.1016/S1573-4463(99)03011-4.

Carothers, T. (2007). How Democracies Emerge: The "Sequencing" Fallacy. *Journal of Democracy, 18*(1), 12–27.

Cerdan-Infantes, P., Makarova, Y., Al-Samarrai, S., & Chen, D. (2013). *Spending More or Spending Better: Improving Education Financing in Indonesia* (Tech. Rep. No. 76404). The World Bank.

Cermeño, A. L., Enflo, K., & Lindvall, J. (2022). Railroads and Reform: How Trains Strengthened the Nation State. *British Journal of Political Science, 52*(2), 1–21. https://doi.org/10.1017/S0007123420000654.

Chang, M. C., Shaeffer, S., Al-Samarrai, S. et al. (2013). *Teacher Reform in Indonesia: The Role of Politics and Evidence in Policy Making* (Tech. Rep. No. 83152). The World Bank.

Coppedge, M., Gerring, J., Knutsen, C. H. et al. (2019). *V-Dem Country-Year Dataset 2019.* Varieties of Democracy (V-Dem) Project. https://doi.org/10.23696/vdemcy19.

Cornell, A., Knutsen, C. H., & Teorell, J. (2020). Bureaucracy and Growth. *Comparative Political Studies, 53*(14), 2246–2282. https://doi.org/10.1177/0010414020912262.

Crouch, H. (1979). Patrimonialism and Military Rule in Indonesia. *World Politics, 31*(4), 571–587. https://doi.org/10.2307/2009910.

Crouch, H. (2010). *Political Reform in Indonesia after Soeharto.* ISEAS.

Cruz, C., & Keefer, P. (2015). Political Parties, Clientelism, and Bureaucratic Reform. *Comparative Political Studies, 48*(14), 1942–1973. https://doi.org/10.1177/0010414015594627.

Dahlstrohm, C., & Lapuente, V. (2017). *Organizing Leviathan: Politicians, Bureaucrats, and the Making of Good Government.* New York: Cambridge University Press.

Dahlum, S., & Knutsen, C. H. (2017). Do Democracies Provide Better Education? Revisiting the Democracy-Human Capital Link. *World Development, 94,* 186–199. https://doi.org/10.1016/j.worlddev.2017.01.001.

Datta, A., Jones, H., Febriany, V. et al. (2011). *The Political Economy of Policy-Making in Indonesia: Opportunities for Improving the Demand for and use of Knowledge* (Working Paper No. 340). ODI.

De Juan, A., Krautwald, F., & Pierskalla, J. H. (2017). Constructing the State: Macro Strategies, Micro Incentives, and the Creation of

Police Forces in Colonial Namibia. *Politics & Society, 45*(2), 269–299. https://doi.org/10.1177/0032329217705352.

de Ree, J., Muralidharan, K., Pradhan, M., & Rogers, H. (2018). Double for Nothing? Experimental Evidence on an Unconditional Teacher Salary Increase in Indonesia. *The Quarterly Journal of Economics, 133*(2), 993–1039. https://doi.org/10.1093/qje/qjx040.

Dincecco, M. (2015). The Rise of Effective States in Europe. *The Journal of Economic History, 75*(3), 901–918. https://doi.org/10.1017/S002205071500114X.

Doner, R. F., Ritchie, B. K., & Slater, D. (2005). Systemic Vulnerability and the Origins of Developmental States: Northeast and Southeast Asia in Comparative Perspective. *International Organization, 59,* 327–361.

Driscoll, B. (2017). Why Political Competition Can Increase Patronage. *Studies in Comparative International Development, 53,* 404–427.

Egorov, G., & Sonin, K. (2011). Dictators and Their Viziers: Endogenizing the Loyalty-Competence Trade-Off. *Journal of the European Economic Association, 9*(5), 903–930. https://doi.org/10.1111/j.1542-4774.2011.01033.x.

Emmerson, D. K. (1983). Understanding the New Order: Bureaucratic Pluralism in Indonesia. *Asian Survey, 25*(11), 1220–1241. https://doi.org/10.2307/2644374.

Erb, M., & Sulistiyanto, P. (Eds.). (2009). *Deepening Democracy in Indonesia? Direct Elections for Local Leaders (Pilkada).* ISEAS.

Evans, P. (1995). *Embedded Autonomy.* Princeton University Press.

Evans, P., & Rauch, J. E. (1999). Bureaucracy and Growth: A CrossNational Analysis of the Effects of "Weberian" State Structures on Economic Growth. *American Sociological Review, 64*(5), 748–765. https://doi.org/10.2307/2657374.

Evers, H.-D. (1987). The Bureaucratization of Southeast Asia. *Comparative Studies in Society and History, 29*(4), 666–685. https://doi.org/10.2307/178821.

Feith, H. (1962). *The Decline of Constitutional Democracy in Indonesia.* Cornell University Press.

Ferraz, C., & Finan, F. (2011). *Motivating Politicians: The Impacts of Monetary Incentives on Quality and Performance.* (Working Paper No. 14906). National Bureau of Economic Research.

Figueroa, V. (2020). Political Corruption Cycles: High-Frequency Evidence from Argentina's Notebooks Scandal. *Comparative Political Studies, 54*(3–4), 482–517. https://doi.org/10.1177/0010414020938102.

Finan, F., Olken, B. A., & Pande, R. (2015). *The Personnel Economics of the State* (Working Paper No. 21825). National Bureau of Economic Research.

Fisman, R. (2001). Estimating the Value of Political Connections. *American Economic Review, 91*(4), 1095–1102.

Franzese, R. (2002). Electoral and Partisan Cycles in Economic Policies and Outcomes. *Annual Review of Political Science, 5,* 369–421.

Fujiwara, T. (2015). Voting Technology, Political Responsiveness, and Infant Health: Evidence From Brazil. *Econometrica, 83*(2), 423–464. https://doi.org/10.3982/ECTA11520.

Geddes, B. (1994). *Politician's Dilemma: Building State Capacity in Latin America.* University of California Press.

Gerring, J., Thacker, S. C., & Alfaro, R. (2012). Democracy and Human Development. *The Journal of Politics, 74*(1), 1–17. https://doi.org/10.1017/S0022381611001113.

Giovanni, C., & Vincenzo, M. (2015). Does Democratization Foster State Consolidation? Democratic Rule, Political Order, and Administrative Capacity. *Governance, 28*(1), 5–24. https://doi.org/10.1111/ gove.12056.

Gjerløw, H., Knutsen, C. H., Wig, T., & Wilson, M. C. (2021). *One Road to Riches? How State Building and Democratization Affect Economic Development.* Elements in Political Economy. Cambridge University Press. https://doi.org/10.1017/9781009053693.

Grindle, M. S. (2012). *Jobs for the Boys: Patronage and the State in Comparative Perspective.* Cambridge, MA: Harvard University Press.

Grundholm, A. T., & Thorsen, M. (2019). Motivated and Able to Make a Difference? The Reinforcing Effects of Democracy and State Capacity on Human Development. *Studies in Comparative International Development, 54*(3), 381–414. https://doi.org/10.1007/s12116-019-09285-2.

Grzymala-Busse, A. (2006). The Discreet Charm of Formal Institutions: Post-communist Party Competition and State Oversight. *Comparative Political Studies, 39*(3), 271–300. https://doi.org/10.1177/0010414005284216.

Grzymala-Busse, A. (2007). *Rebuilding Leviathan: Party Competition and State Exploitation in Post-Communist Democracies.* Cambridge University Press.

Gueorguiev, D. D., & Schuler, P. (2016). Keeping Your Head Down: Public Profiles and Promotion under Autocracy. *Journal of East Asian Studies, 16*(1), 87–116.

Gulzar, S., & Pasquale, B. J. (2017). Politicians, Bureaucrats, and Development: Evidence from India. *American Political Science Review, 111*(1), 162–183. https://doi.org/10.1017/S0003055416000502.

Hadiz, V. R. (2010). *Localising Power in Post-Authoritarian Indonesia: A Southeast Asia Perspective.* Stanford University Press.

Hanson, J. K. (2015). Democracy and State Capacity: Complements or Substitutes? *Studies in Comparative International Development, 50*(3), 304–330. https://doi.org/10.1007/s12116-014-9173-z.

Hanson, J. K., & Sigman, R. (2021). Leviathan's Latent Dimensions: Measuring State Capacity for Comparative Political Research. *The Journal of Politics, 83*(4), 1495–1510. https://doi.org/10.1086/715066.

Hanusch, M., & Keefer, P. (2013). *Promises, Promises: Vote-Buying and the Electoral Mobilization Strategies of Non-Credible Politicians.* (Working Paper No. 6653). World Bank Policy Research.

Harding, R. (2019). Who is Democracy Good For? Elections, Rural Bias, and Health and Education Outcomes in Sub-Saharan Africa. *The Journal of Politics, 82*(1), 241–254. https://doi.org/10.1086/705745.

Harding, R., & Stasavage, D. (2014). What Democracy Does (and Doesn't Do) for Basic Services: School Fees, School Inputs, and African Elections. *The Journal of Politics, 76*(1), 229–245.

Hasnain, Z., Manning, N., & Pierskalla, J. H. (2014). The Promise of Performance Pay? Reasons for Caution in Policy Prescriptions in the Core Civil Service. *The World Bank Research Observer, 29*(2), 235–264. https://doi.org/10.1093/wbro/lku001.

Hassan, M. (2020). *Regime Threats and State Solutions: Bureaucreatic Loyalty and Embeddedness in Kenya.* New York: Cambridge University Press.

He, G., & Wang, S. (2017). Do College Graduates Serving as Village Officials Help Rural China? *American Economic Journal: Applied Economics, 9*(4), 186–215. https://doi.org/10.1257/app.20160079.

Hendrix, C. (2010). Measuring State Capacity: Theoretical and Empirical Implications for the Study of Civil Conflict. *Journal of Peace Research, 47*(3), 273–285.

Hicken, A. (2011). Clientelism. *Annual Review of Political Science, 14*, 289–310.

Horn, M. J. (1995). *The Political Economy of Public Administration: Institutional Choice in the Public Sector.* Cambridge University Press.

Huang, C.-H., & Kang, D. C. (2022). State Formation in Korea and Japan, 400-800 CE: Emulation and Learning, Not Bellicist Competition. *International Organization, 76*(1), 1–31. https://doi.org/10.1017/S0020818321000254.

Huntington, S. P. (1968). *Political Order in Changing Societies.* Yale University Press.

Jia, R., Kudamatsu, M., & Seim, D. (2015). Political Selection in China: The Complementary Roles of Connections and Performance. *Journal of the European Economic Association, 13*(4), 631–668. https://doi.org/10.1111/jeea.12124.

Jiang, J. (2018). Making Bureaucracy Work: Patronage Networks, Performance Incentives, and Economic Development in China. *American Journal of Political Science, 62*(4), 982–999. https://doi.org/10.1111/ajps.12394.

Jiang, J., Shao, Z., & Zhang, Z. (2022). The Price of Probity: Anticorruption and Adverse Selection in the Chinese Bureaucracy. *British Journal of Political Science, 52*(1), 1–24. https://doi.org/10.1017/S0007123420000393.

Karachiwalla, N., & Park, A. (2017). Promotion Incentives in the Public Sector: Evidence from Chinese Schools. *Journal of Public Economics, 146*, 109–128. https://doi.org/10.1016/j.jpubeco.2016.12.004.

Keefer, P. (2007). Clientelism, Credibility, and the Policy Choices of Young Democracies. *American Journal of Political Science, 51*(4), 804–821. https://doi.org/10.1111/j.1540-5907.2007.00282.x.

Keefer, P., & Vlaicu, R. (2007). Democracy, Credibility, and Clientelism. *Journal of Law, Economics & Organization, 24*(2), 371–406.

Kemahlioglu, O. (2011). Jobs in Politicians' Backyards: Party Leadership Competition and Patronage. *Journal of Theoretical Politics, 23*(4), 480–509.

Khemani, S. (2004). Political Cycles in a Developing Economy: Effect of Elections in the Indian States. *Journal of Development Economics, 73*, 125–154.

Kis-Katos, K., & Sjahrir, B. S. (2017). The Impact of Fiscal and Political Decentralization on Local Public Investment in Indonesia. *Journal of Comparative Economics, 45*(2), 344–365. https://doi.org/10.1016/j.jce.2017.03.003.

Kitschelt, H., & Wilkinson, S. I. (2007). Citizen-Politician Linkages: An Introduction. In H. Kitschelt & S. I. Wilkinson (Eds.), *Patrons: Clients, and Policies. Patterns of Democratic Accountability and Political Competition* (pp. 1–49). Cambridge University Press.

Kohli, A. (2004). *State-Directed Development: Political Power and Industrialization in the Global Periphery.* Cambridge University Press.

Kristiansen, S., & Ramli, M. (2006). Buying an Income: The Market for Civil Service Positions in Indonesia. *Contemporary Southeast Asia: A Journal of International and Strategic Affairs, 28*(2), 207–233.

Kudamatsu, M. (2012). Has Democratization Reduced Infant Mortality in Sub-Saharan Africa? Evidence from Micro Data. *Journal of the European*

Economic Association, 10(6), 1294–1317. https://doi.org/10.1111/j.1542-4774.2012.01092.x.

LaForge, G. (2016). Changing a Civil Service Culture: Reforming Indonesia's Ministry of Finance, 2006–2010. Princeton University Case Study. https://successfulsocieties.princeton.edu/sites/successfulsocieties/files/GL_CC_Indonesia_MOF_FORMATTED_5May2016.pdf

Landry, P. F., Lü, X., & Duan, H. (2018). Does Performance Matter? Evaluating Political Selection Along the Chinese Administrative Ladder. *Comparative Political Studies, 51*(8), 1074–1105. https://doi.org/10.1177/0010414017730078.

Lee, D. S., & Schuler, P. (2020). Testing the "China Model" of Meritocratic Promotions: Do Democracies Reward Less Competent Ministers Than Autocracies? *Comparative Political Studies, 55*(3–4), 531–566. https://doi.org/10.1177/0010414019858962.

Lee, M. M., & Zhang, N. (2016). Legibility and the Informational Foundations of State Capacity. *The Journal of Politics, 79*(1), 118–132. https://doi.org/10.1086/688053.

Levitsky, S., & Way, L. A. (2010). *Competitive Authoritarianism: Hybrid Regimes after the Cold War.* Cambridge University Press.

Lewis, B. D. (2005). Indonesian Local Government Spending, Taxing and Saving: An Explanation of Pre- and Post-decentralization Fiscal Outcomes. *Asian Economic Journal, 19,* 291–317.

Lewis, B. D. (2017). Does Local Government Proliferation Improve Public Service Delivery? Evidence from Indonesia. *Journal of Urban Affairs, 39*(8), 1047–1065. https://doi.org/10.1080/07352166.2017.1323544.

Liddle, R. W. (1985). Soeharto's Indonesia: Personal Rule and Political Institutions. *Pacific Affairs, 55*(1), 68–90. https://doi.org/10.2307/2758010.

Liddle, R. W. (1987). The Politics of Shared Growth: Some Indonesian Cases. *Comparative Politics, 19*(2), 127–146.

Lindsey, T. (2019). A Requiem for Reformasi as Joko Widodo Unravels Indonesia's Democratic Legacy. *The Conversation.*

Logsdon, M. G. (1992). Indonesia's Civil Service in the New Order: Consolidation, Growth, and Change. *Sojourn: Journal of Social Issues in Southeast Asia, 7*(2), 223–247.

Mackie, J. (2010). Patrimonialism: The New Order and Beyond. In E. Aspinall & G. Fealy (Eds.), *Soehartos New Order and Its Legacy: Essays in Honor of Harold Crouch* (p. 81–98). Canberra: ANU Press.

Mann, M. (1984). The Autonomous Power of the State: Its Origins, Mechanisms and Results. *European Journal of Sociology, 25*(2), 185–213.

Mann, M. (1986). *The Sources of Social Power. Volume 1: A History of Power From the Beginning to AD 1760.* New York: Cambridge University Press.

Martinez-Bravo, M. (2017). The Local Political Economy Effects of School Construction in Indonesia. *American Economic Journal: Applied Economics, 9*(2), 256–289. https://doi.org/10.1257/app.20150447.

McIntyre, A. (2005). *The Indonesian Presidency: The Shift From Personal Toward Constitutional Rule.* Rowman & Littlefield.

McLeod, R. H. (2000). Soeharto's Indonesia: A Better Class of Corruption. *Agenda: A Journal of Policy Analysis and Reform, 7*(2), 99–112. https://doi.org/10.2307/43199068.

McLeod, R. H. (2008). Inadequate Budgets and Salaries as Instruments for Institutionalizing Public Sector Corruption in Indonesia. *South East Asia Research, 16*(2), 199–223.

McVey, R. (1982). The Beamtenstaat in Indonesia. In B. Anderson & A. Kahin (Eds.), *Interpreting Indonesian Politics: Thirteen Contributions to the Debate* (pp. 84–91). Ithaca, NY: Cornell University Press.

Meyer-Sahling, J.-H., Mikkelsen, K. S., & Schuster, C. (2018). Civil Service Management and Corruption: What We Know and What We Don't. *Public Administration, 96*(2), 276–285. https://doi.org/10.1111/padm.12404.

Mietzner, M. (2014). *Money, Power, and Ideology: Political Parties in Post Authoritarian Indonesia.* Asian Studies Association of Australia.

Mietzner, M. (2015). *Reinventing Asian Populism: Jokowi's Rise, Democracy, and Political Contestation in Indonesia* (Tech. Rep. No. 72). East-West Center.

Mietzner, M. (2018a). Authoritarian Elections, State Capacity, and Performance Legitimacy: Phases of Regime Consolidation and Decline in Suharto's Indonesia. *International Political Science Review, 39*(1), 83–96. https://doi.org/10.1177/0192512116687139.

Mietzner, M. (2018b). Indonesia: Why Democratization Has Not Reduced Corruption. In *Handbook on the Geographies of Corruption.* (pp. 350–364). Elgaronline.

Muhtadi, B. (2019). *Vote Buying in Indonesia: The Mechanics of Electoral Bribery.* Palgrave Macmillan.

Nuswantoro, H. (2017). Does the Implementation of a Formal Performance Management System Improve Employee Performance? Perspectives from Indonesian Civil Servants (Unpublished Master's Thesis). Melbounre School of Government.

O'Dwyer, C. (2004). Runaway State Building: How Political Parties Shape States in Postcommunist Eastern Europe. *World Politics, 56*(4), 520–553. https://doi.org/10.1353/wp.2005.0007.

OECD, & Asian Development Bank. (2019). *Government at a Glance Southeast Asia 2019* (Tech. Rep.). https://doi.org/10.1787/9789264305915-en.

Oliveros, V. (2021). Working for the Machine. Patronage Jobs and Political Services in Argentina. *Comparative Politics, 53*(3), 381–427.

Oliveros, V. (2021). *Patronage at Work.* Cambridge University Press.

Olson, M. (1993). Dictatorship, Democracy, and Development. *American Political Science Review, 87*(3), 567–576.

Pemstein, D., Tzelgov, E., & Wang, Y.-t. (2015). *Evaluating and Improving Item Response Theory Models for Cross-National Expert Surveys* (SSRN Scholarly Paper No. ID 2613421). Social Science Research Network. https://doi.org/10.2139/ssrn.2613421.

Pepinsky, T. (2007). Autocracy, Elections, and Fiscal Policy: Evidence from Malaysia. *Studies in Comparative International Development, 42*(1), 136–163. https://doi.org/10.1007/s12116-007-9006-4.

Pepinsky, T. (2009). *Economic Crises and the Breakdown of Authoritarian Regimes: Indonesia and Malaysia in Comparative Perspective.* Cambridge University Press.

Pepinsky, T. B. (2007). *Financial Crises, Capital Controls, and Authoritarian Breakdowns.* Cambridge University Press.

Pepinsky, T. B., Pierskalla, J. H., & Sacks, A. (2017). Bureaucracy and Service Delivery. *Annual Review of Political Science, 20,* 249–268.

Pepinsky, T. B., & Wihardja, M. M. (2011). Decentralization and Economic Performance in Indonesia. *Journal of East Asian Studies, 11*(3), 337–371. https://doi.org/10.1017/S1598240800007372.

Perry, J. L., & Hondegheim, A. (Eds.). (2008). *Motivation in Public Management: The Call of Public Service.* Oxford University Press.

Pierskalla, J. H. (2016). Splitting the Difference? The Politics of District Creation in Indonesia. *Comparative Politics, 48*(2), 249–268. https://doi.org/10.5129/001041516817037754.

Pierskalla, J. H., Lauretig, A., Rosenberg, A. S., & Sacks, A. (2021). Democratization and Representative Bureaucracy: An Analysis of Promotion Patterns in Indonesia's Civil Service, 1980–2015. *American Journal of Political Science, 65*(2), 261–277. https://doi.org/10.1111/ajps.12536.

Pierskalla, J. H., & Sacks, A. (2017). Unpacking the Effect of Decentralized Governance on Routine Violence: Lessons from Indonesia. *World Development, 90,* 213–228. https://doi.org/10.1016/j.worlddev.2016.09.008.

Pierskalla, J. H., & Sacks, A. (2018). Unpaved Road Ahead: The Consequences of Election Cycles for Capital Expenditures. *The Journal of Politics, 80*(2), 510–524. https://doi.org/10.1086/694547.

Pierskalla, J. H., & Sacks, A. (2020). Personnel Politics: Elections, Clientelistic Competition and Teacher Hiring in Indonesia. *British Journal of Political Science, 50*(4), 1283–1305. https://doi.org/10.1017/S0007123418000601.

Pramusinto, A. (2016). Weak Central Authority and Fragmented Bureaucracy: A Study of Policy Implementation in Indonesia. In J. S. Quah (Ed.), *The Role of the Public Bureaucracy in Policy Implementation in Five ASEAN Countries* (pp. 98–170). Cambridge University Press.

Quah, J. S. T. (Ed.). (2016). *The Role of the Public Bureaucracy in Policy Implementation in Five ASEAN Countries.* Cambridge University Press. https://doi.org/10.1017/CBO9781316340653.

Raadschelders, J. C., Vigoda-Gadot, E., & Kisner, M. (2015). *Global Dimensions of Public Administration and Governance.* Hoboken, NJ: John Wiley.

Rauch, J. E., & Evans, P. B. (2000). Bureaucratic Structure and Bureaucratic Performance in Less Developed Countries. *Journal of Public Economics, 75*(1), 49–71. https://doi.org/10.1016/S0047-2727(99)00044-4.

Reuter, O. J., & Robertson, G. B. (2012). Subnational Appointments in Authoritarian Regimes: Evidence from Russian Gubernatorial Appointments. *Journal of Politics, 74*(4), 1023–1037.

Robison, R., & Hadiz, V. (2004). *Reorganising Power in Indonesia: The Politics of Oligarchy in an Age of Markets.* Routledge.

Rogoff, K. (1990). Equilibrium Political Business Cycles. *American Economic Review, 80*, 21–36.

Roosa, J. (2006). *Pretext for Mass Murder: The September 30th Movement & Suharto's Coup d'Etat in Indonesia.* University of Wisconsin Press.

Ross, M. (2006). Is Democracy Good for the Poor? *American Journal of Political Science, 50*(4), 860–874. https://doi.org/10.1111/j.1540-5907.2006.00220.x.

Rosser, A., & Fahmi, M. (2016). *The Political Economy of Teacher Management in Decentralized Indonesia* (Working Paper No. 7913). World Bank Policy Research.

Rosser, A., & Sulistiyanto, P. (2013). The Politics of Universal Free Basic Education in Decentralized Indonesia: Insights from Yogyakarta. *Pacific Affairs, 86*(3), 539–560. https://doi.org/10.5509/2013863539.

Ruhil, A. V. S., & Camões, P. J. (2003). What Lies Beneath: The Political Roots of State Merit Systems. *Journal of Public Administration Research and Theory, 13*(1), 27–42. https://doi.org/10.1093/jpart/mug006.

Saez, L., & Sinha, A. (2010). Political Cycles, Political Institutions and Public Expenditure in India, 1980–2000. *British Journal of Political Science, 40*(1), 91–113.

Sandefur, J., & Wadhwa, D. (2018). Chart of the Week #3: Why the World Bank Should Ditch the "Doing Business" Rankings – in One Embarrassing Chart. *Center for Global Development.*

Scharpf, A., & Gläßel, C. (2020). Why Underachievers Dominate Secret Police Organizations: Evidence from Autocratic Argentina. *American Journal of Political Science, 64*(4), 791–806. https://doi.org/10.1111/ajps.12475.

Schuster, C. (2017). Legal Reform Need Not Come First: Merit-Based Civil Service Management in Law and Practice. *Public Administration, 95*(3), 571–588. https://doi.org/10.1111/padm.12334.

Schuster, C. (2020). Patrons against Clients: Electoral Uncertainty and Bureaucratic Tenure in Politicized States. *Regulation & Governance, 14*(1), 26–43. https://doi.org/10.1111/rego.12186.

Scott, J. C. (2017). *Against the Grain: A Deep History of the Earliest States.* Yale University Press.

Shandra, J. M., Nobles, J., London, B., & Williamson, J. B. (2003). Dependency, Democracy, and Infant Mortality: A Quantitative, Cross-National Analysis of Less Developed Countries. *Social Science and Medicine, 59*(2), 321–333.

Shih, V., Adolph, C., & Liu, M. (2012). Getting Ahead in the Communist Party: Explaining the Advancement of Central Committee Members in China. *American Political Science Review, 106*(1), 166–187. https://doi.org/10.1017/S0003055411000566.

Sjahrir, B. S., Kis-Katos, K., & Schulze, G. (2013). Political Budget Cycles in Indonesia at the District Level. *Economics Letters, 120*(2), 342–345.

Skoufias, E., Narayan, A., Dasgupta, B., & Kaiser, K. (2014). *Electoral Accountability and Local Government Spending in Indonesia.* The World Bank.

Slater, D. (2008). Can Leviathan be Democratic? Competitive Elections, Robust Mass Politics, and State Infrastructural Power. *Studies in Comparative International Development, 43*(3), 252–272. https://doi.org/10.1007/ s12116-008-9026-8.

Slater, D., & Simmons, E. (2013). Coping by Colluding Political Uncertainty and Promiscuous Powersharing in Indonesia and Bolivia. *Comparative Political Studies, 46*(11), 1366–1393. https://doi.org/10.1177/0010414012453447.

Soifer, H. (2008). State Infrastructural Power: Approaches to Conceptualization and Measurement. *Studies in Comparative International Development, 43*(3–4), 231. https://doi.org/10.1007/s12116-008-9028-6.

Stasavage, D. (2005). Democracy and Education Spending in Africa. *American Journal of Political Science, 49*(2), 343–358. https://doi.org/10.1111/j.0092-5853 .2005.00127.x.

Stasavage, D. (2020). *The Decline and Rise of Democracy: A Global History from Antiquity to Today.* Princeton University Press.

Sumampouw, N. S. (2016). North Sulawesi: Clan, Church and State. In E. Aspinall & M. Sukmajati (Eds.), *Electoral Dynamics in Indonesia: Money Politics, Patronage and Clientelism at the Grassroots* (pp. 321–340). Singapore: National University of Singapore Press.

Suwitri, S., Supriyono, B., & Kuswandaru, O. (2019). Transactional Politics in Filling High leadership Positions in Indonesian Bureaucratic Organizations. *International Journal of Research in Humanities and Social Studies, 6*(5), 38–50.

Svolik, M. W. (2012). *The Politics of Authoritarian Rule.* Cambridge University Press.

Svolik, M. W. (2013). Contracting on Violence: The Moral Hazard in Authoritarian Repression and Military Intervention in Politics. *Journal of Conflict Resolution, 57*(5), 765–794. https://doi.org/10.1177/0022002712449327.

Theriault, S. M. (2003). Patronage, the Pendleton Act, and the Power of the People. *Journal of Politics, 65*(1), 50–68. https://doi.org/10.1111/ 1468-2508.t01-1-00003.

Tidey, S. (2012). Performing the State: Everyday Practices, Corruption and Reciprocity in Middle Indonesian Civil Service (Unpublished Doctoral Dissertation). University of Amsterdam.

Tilly, C. (1990). *Coercion, Capital, and European States, AD 990–1990.* Oxford: Blackwell.

Ting, M. M., Snyder, J. M., Hirano, S., & Folke, O. (2013). Elections and Reform: The Adoption of Civil Service Systems in the U.S. States. *Journal of Theoretical Politics, 25*(3), 363–387. https://doi.org/10.1177/0951629812453217.

Tjiptoherijanto, P. (2007). Civil Service Reform in Indonesia. *International Public Management Review, 8*(2), 31–44.

Tjiptoherijanto, P. (2014). *Reform of the Indonesian Civil Service: Racing with Decentralization* (Working Paper No. 02/2014).

Tjiptoherijanto, P. (2018). Reform of the Indonesian Civil Service: Looking for Quality. *Economics World, 6*(6), 433–443. https://doi.org/10.17265/2328-7144/2018.06.002.

Tomsa, D. (2015). Local Politics and Corruption in Indonesia's Outer Islands. *Bijdragen tot de Taal-, Land- en Volkenkunde, 171*(2/3), 196–219.

Toral, G. (2019). *Political Bureaucratic Cycles: How Politicians' Responses to Electoral Incentives and Anti-Corruption Policies Disrupt the Bureaucracy and Service Delivery Around Elections* (Working Paper). https://ic3jm.es/wp-content/uploads/2021/10/benefits_of_patronage.pdf.

Toral, G. (2021). *The Benefits of Patronage: How the Political Appointment of Bureaucrats Can Enhance Their Accountability and Effectiveness* (Working Paper). https://ic3jm.es/wp-content/uploads/2021/10/benefits_of_patronage.pdf.

Valsecchi, M. (2016). *Corrupt Bureaucrats: The Response of Non-Elected Officials to Electoral Accountability* (Working Paper). https://ideas.repec.org/p/hhs/gunwpe/0684.html

Vatikiotis, M. R. J. (1998). *Indonesian Politics under Suharto: The Rise and Fall of the New Order.* Psychology Press.

Vickers, A. (2005). *A History of Modern Indonesia.* Cambridge University Press.

Voth, H.-J., & Xu, G. (2020). *Discretion and Destruction: Promotions, Performance and Patronage in the Royal Navy* (Working Paper). http://guoxu.org/docs/DiscretionNavy_Nov20.pdf.

Wang, E., & Xu, Y. (2018). Awakening Leviathan: The Effect of Democracy on State Capacity. *Research & Politics, 5*(2).

Warburton, E. (2016). Southeast Sulawesi: Money Politics in Indonesia's Nickel Belt. In E. Aspinall & M. Sukmajati (Eds.), *Electoral Dynamics in Indonesia: Money Politics, Patronage and Clientelism at the Grassroots* (pp. 341–362). Singapore: National University of Singapore Press.

Warwick, D. P. (1987). The Effectiveness of the Indonesian Civil Service. *Southeast Asian Journal of Social Science, 15*(2), 40–56. https://doi.org/10.2307/24491121.

Weaver, J. (2021). Jobs for Sale: Corruption and Misallocation in Hiring. *American Economic Review, 111*(10), 3093–3122. https://doi.org/10.1257/aer.20201062.

Weber, M. (1978). *Economy and Society.* University of California Press.

Weitz-Shapiro, R. (2012). What Wins Votes: Why Some Politicians Opt Out of Clientelism. *American Journal of Political Science, 56*(3), 568–583. https://doi.org/10.1111/j.1540-5907.2011.00578.x.

World Bank. (2003). *Decentralizing Indonesia: A Regional Public Expenditure Review.*

Xu, C. (2011). The Fundamental Institutions of China's Reforms and Development. *Journal of Economic Literature, 49*(4), 1076–1151. https://doi.org/10.1257/jel.49.4.1076.

Zakharov, A. V. (2016). The Loyalty-Competence Trade-Off in Dictatorships and Outside Options for Subordinates. *The Journal of Politics, 78*(2), 457–466. https://doi.org/10.1086/684365.

Zudenkova, G. (2015). Political Cronyism. *Social Choice and Welfare, 44*(3), 473–492. https://doi.org/10.1007/s00355-014-0854-3.

Acknowledgements

This work has benefited tremendously from the valuable feedback of Ben Olken, Michael Callen, Guo Xu, Horatio Larreguy, Priya Mukherjee, Daniel Rogger, Erwin Ariadharma, Lily Hoo, Dewi Susanti, Nils Weidmann, Bill Liddle, Martin Williams, Saad Gulzar, Mai Hassan, Dan Honig, Kate Baldwin, Dan Mattingly, SP Harish, Zahid Hasnain, Guy Grossman, Erik Wibbels, Thad Dunning, participants at the ESTA Workshop at the University of Konstanz, seminar participants at OSU, seminar participants at Yale University, workshop participants at Johns Hopkins, brownbag participants at the World Bank, and seminar participants at William & Mary, UIUC, Cornell University, and NYU Abu Dhabi. I am indebted to BKN, for sharing their data and collaborating on this project, to Audrey Sacks, Yulia Herawati, and team from the World Bank's Social Development Program for cleaning and putting together the dataset, Adam Lauretig, Drew Rosenberg, Jianzi He, and Cara D'Alesio for exceptional research assistance, and to the ASC Unity cluster staff who helped troubleshoot OSU's cluster computing resources.

Cambridge Elements ≡

Political Economy

David Stasavage
New York University

David Stasavage is Julius Silver Professor in the Wilf Family Department of Politics at New York University. He previously held positions at the London School of Economics and at Oxford University. His work has spanned a number of different fields and currently focuses on two areas: development of state institutions over the long run and the politics of inequality. He is a member of the American Academy of Arts and Sciences.

About the Series

The Element Series Political Economy provides authoritative contributions on important topics in the rapidly growing field of political economy. Elements are designed so as to provide broad and in-depth coverage combined with original insights from scholars in political science, economics, and economic history. Contributions are welcome on any topic within this field.

Cambridge Elements ≡

Political Economy

Elements in the Series

State Capacity and Economic Development: Present and Past
Mark Dincecco

Nativism and Economic Integration Across the Developing World: Collision and Accommodation
Rikhil R. Bhavnani, Bethany Lacina

Reform and Rebellion in Weak States
Evgeny Finkel, Scott Gehlbach

Lynching and Local Justice
Danielle F. Jung, Dara Kay Cohen

The Economic Origin of Political Parties
Christopher Kam, Adlai Newson

Backsliding
Stephan Haggard, Robert Kaufman

A Moral Political Economy
Federica Carugati, Margaret Levi

One Road to Riches?
Haakon Gjerløw, Tore Wig, Carl Henrik Knutsen, Matthew Charles Wilson

Democratization and the State
Jan H. Pierskalla

A full series listing is available at: www.cambridge.org/EPEC

Printed in the United States
by Baker & Taylor Publisher Services